GWG: Piece by Piece

CATHERINE C. COLE

Piece by Piece

GOOSE LANE

The author wishes to thank to the Alberta Historical Resources Foundation for funding to support the writing of this manuscript. Funding and other support for earlier stages of this work were provided by the Alberta Historical Resources Foundation, the Alberta Museums Association, the Edmonton Community Foundation, the University of Alberta, D.Active Productions, the Edmonton Cultural Capital Community Arts Program, City of Edmonton/Department of Canadian Heritage, the Alberta Labour History Institute, the Provincial Archives of Alberta, the Royal Alberta Museum, and the Virtual Museum of Canada.

Goose Lane Editions acknowledges the financial support of the Canada Council for the Arts, the Government of Canada through the Canada Book Fund (CBF), and the government of New Brunswick through the Department of Wellness, Culture, and Sport.

Edited by Rebecca Leaman.
Cover photo by Lucie Heins.
Cover and book design by Jaye Haworth.
Art direction by Julie Scriver.
Printed in Canada.
10 9 8 7 6 5 4 3 2 1

Library and Archives Canada Cataloguing in Publication

Cole, Catherine C. (Catherine Cooper), 1958-
    GWG: piece by piece / Catherine C. Cole.

Includes bibliographical references and index.
ISBN 978-0-86492-641-8

1. G.W.G. (Firm) — History.
2. Clothing factories — Canada — History 20th century.
3. Clothing trade — Canada.
4. Clothing workers — Canada — History — 20th century.
5. Industrial relations — Canada — History — 20th century. I. Title.
HD9940.C34G73 2012   338.7'6870971   C2011-902886-7

Goose Lane Editions
500 Beaverbrook Court, Suite 330
Fredericton, New Brunswick
CANADA E3B 5X4
www.gooselane.com

To the former employees of the
Great Western Garment Company

9   **PREFACE**
The Piece by Piece Project

11   **ACKNOWLEDGEMENTS**

15   **INTRODUCTION**
An Edmonton Company 16

19   **CHAPTER ONE 1911-1929**
Unionization 20
    Marketing to Labour 22
The Garment District 24
"Made in the West for the West" 26
Working Conditions 30
"They Wear Longer Because They're Made Stronger" 35
Minimum Wage 35
    Expansion of the GWG Plant 41

53   **CHAPTER TWO 1930-1939**
Cowboy Kings 54
The Stevens Commission 59
    GWG Brands 64

87   **CHAPTER THREE 1939-1946**
"Fighting Hitler with Needles" 93
    Clarence D. Jacox, 1945 93
Working Conditions 98
    A Day in the Life of the Factory 102
Worth Waiting For 102
    How to Identify GWG Clothing 108

113   **CHAPTER FOUR 1946-1961**
    Doug Stephens, 1918-1972 119
"Featured at Leading Stores across Canada" 124
Workers on the Move 124
Industrial Nursing 130
    Emily Ross, Union Activist 131
Challenges Ahead 133

Anne Baranyk, President of Local 120 UGWA, 1956-1970 134
The Last Best West 136
Cowboy Up! 140
Marketing to Canadian Families 146

151   **CHAPTER FIVE 1962-1986**
Foreign Competition and Ownership   152
Increasingly Diverse Workforce   156
Kitchen-Peabody   160
Winnipeg Pants   160
Foreign Competition   161
The Youth Market   164
Bought Out by Levi Strauss   165
Consolidation   169
Anne Ozipko   170
Great Northern Apparel   170
Parlez-vous français?   173
Wayne Gretzky Really did Grow Up in GWGs, 1981   177

179   **CHAPTER SIX 1986-2004**
Workers from Twenty-Seven Different Countries   179
Occupational Health and Safety   183
English in the Workplace   185
Levis Strauss Absorbed GWG   187
The End of Piecework   188
"I Saw My Manager Cry"   193
A Lasting Legacy   194
GWG Catalogues   195
How to Make a Pair of Jeans   200

205   **NOTES ON SOURCES**

207   **INDEX**

This book is part of a larger undertaking called Piece by Piece, a multidimensional project that in 2004 began to document and explore the history of the Great Western Garment Company (GWG) through different media, including:

GWG: Piece by Piece, a sixty-minute musical multi-media piece created by singer/songwriter Maria Dunn and filmmaker Don Bouzek of Ground Zero Productions, depicting the experiences of immigrant women who worked in Edmonton's GWG clothing factory over its ninety-three-year history. http://www.MariaDunn.com

Piece by Piece: The GWG Story, a virtual exhibition about the history of GWG that includes information for teachers, collectors, and researchers, and integrates a number of video excerpts from oral history interviews, developed by the Royal Alberta Museum (RAM) in partnership with the Provincial Archives of Alberta (PAA), the Alberta Labour History Institute, D.Active Productions, and Catherine C. Cole & Associates with funding from the Virtual Museum of Canada. http://www.royalalbertamuseum.ca/virtualExhibit/GWG/en/index.html

Commemoration of the Chartering of Local 120 of the United Garment Workers of America at the Great Western Garment Company as an event of national historic significance by the Historic Sites and Monuments Board of Canada.

Collections development, including a large collection of artifacts now at the Royal Alberta Museum, the Local 120 UGWA Collection at the Provincial Archives of Alberta, and an extensive collection of oral histories conducted with former employees of GWG and Levi Strauss.

A number of temporary displays and public presentations.

I wrote this book at the instigation of retired workers, who marvelled at my interest in the Great Western Garment Company and greeted me with, "So you're the lady writing the book about GWG." Eventually, I had to agree.

ACKNOWLEDGEMENTS

My recent interest in the history of GWG was awakened nearly ten years ago when collector Ray Elliott approached me about work he was doing to prepare a collectors' guide to vintage GWG. Ray had accumulated a large collection of vintage clothing. Spurred on by his interest, I started collecting GWG advertisements, catalogues, giveaways, and to a lesser degree clothing—casually at first.

Filmmaker Don Bouzek of D.Active Productions approached me about collaborating on a video ballad project about the immigrant workers at GWG as a one hundredth anniversary project for either the city's (2004) or the province's centennial (2005). I had studied the early history of the company in graduate school but knew little about the postwar period. It has been a real pleasure to collaborate with Don on the Piece by Piece project.

Then I met Ian McDonald, an eBay pen pal and former Red Strap wearer, who shared my enthusiasm for the minutiae about GWG products and marketing, and has been very helpful.

My husband, Gordon Wood, and children Jessica, Stirling, Murray, and Richard, spent countless hours looking for GWG material, listening to GWG stories, and occasionally trying on garments from the growing collection. They sustained my interest through the years.

I would also like to thank Cathy Roy, Curator of Western Canadian History at the Royal Alberta Museum (RAM), for her ongoing encouragement, and the virtual exhibition team for their enthusiasm, particularly: editor Lou Morin, Bryan Kulba and Stephan Duret of Kobot Industries Digital Media, Matthias Reinicke, Lime Design, and Jessica King, Program/Volunteer Coordinator, Provincial Archives of Alberta (PAA).

Levi Strauss generously allowed us to document manufacturing processes in the Edmonton plant in the weeks before the plant closed and introduced researchers to plant workers willing to be interviewed. During an earlier phase of this research in the mid-1980s, when GWG was working on its own history for the seventy-fifth anniversary, the company gave me access to archival records for the pre-war era in the Great Northern Apparel offices in Richmond Hill, Ontario. However, I did not have access to more recent company records following the closure of the plant.

I would like to thank Local 120G UFCW (formerly UGWA), particularly Giuseppina Tagliente and Janet Cardinal, for providing access to their archival records and members, and to Anne Ozipko for inviting me to the seventy-fifth anniversary banquet in 1986 and introducing me to many early plant workers who I was able to interview at that time.

Thanks to Lan Chan Marples and Mary Fung who conducted interviews in Chinese. Joan Schiebelbein and Maria Dunn assisted with a number of the interviews. Don Bouzek and Randy Robinson filmed the interviews and the closing days in the factory. Andrena Shaw took the still photographs at the plant. Edmonton Mennonite Centre for Newcomers staff, particularly Beverly Walker and Judy Sillito, identified people to interview.

Susan Gamble of the *Brantford Expositor* wrote a column about the project encouraging former workers and their families to come forward and provided access to the paper's morgue. The Brant Historical Society and the Brantford Public Library provided information about the Brantford plants.

Victoria Lamb Drover conducted research on the history of the plant in Saskatoon. Ruth Bitner of the Western Development Museum, Patrick Hayes at the University of Saskatchewan Archives, the staff of the Saskatoon Local History Room, and Jeff O'Brien at the Saskatoon City Archives provided information about the Saskatoon plant.

Murray Peterson provided input into the history of the company in Winnipeg. Keith B. Smith and Louise Duguay assisted in interpreting commercial art.

Nichole Quiring conducted some of the early research.

Lucie Bettez conducted research on GWG and the French-Canadian market.

In Alberta, thanks to Leslie Latta Guthrie, Director; Marlena Wyman, former Audio Visual Archivist; and Irene Jendzjowsky, Director, Access and Preservation Services, all with the Provincial Archives of Alberta; Kathryn Ivany and Michael Payne of the City of Edmonton Archives; and Lucie Heins, Assistant Curator, Western Canadian History, Royal Alberta Museum provided access to images and artifacts in their collections.

Kirsti Tamblyn, Ariane Lemire, and Randy Robinson of D.Active, Katie Roth and Dennis Hyduk at the Provincial Archives of Alberta scanned the photographs and catalogues. Archivists and librarians at Library and Archives Canada, the Glenbow Archives, the Calgary Stampede Archives, and Edmonton Public Library and University of Alberta Library provided valuable assistance.

I would like to thank the many former employees of GWG and Levi Strauss who agreed to be interviewed or provided information, artifacts, or photographs during this study, a number of whom have now sadly passed away:

Edmonton: Helen Allan (née Schwindt), Max Bedard, Merlin Beharry, Jean Binette, Kulminder Bolina, Susan Bui, Anne Broad (née Baranyk), Janet Cardinal, Mee Chan, Assunta Dotto, Nellie Engley, Don Freeland, Emma Gilbertson, Georgina Graff, Eileen Hatch, Barb Heath, Hilary Hellum, Norah Hook, Zi Hua Hu, Sadat Khan, Bhubinder Kullar, Meena Jassal, Louis Kabesh, Shirley Law, Suet Lee, Chee Luck Mah, Jo-Anne Mack, Hang Sau Mah, Julie Mah, Virginia Mah, Lillian Morris, Kim Ngo, Joyce Nimrichter, Anne Ozipko, Dale Pearn, Hana Razga, Annette Richardson, Bob Robinson, Mary Romanuk, Virginia Sauve, Elizabeth Shinbine, Sarojni Siwami, Giuseppina Tagliente, Chris Tigeris, Sum Yuk Wong, Tommy Wong, Elizabeth Kozma, Emily Waggott (née Gale), Beverly Walker, Beulah Williams (née Nelson), Ilene Yeandle, and Lillian Wasylynchuk.

Brantford: Brenda Bridgewater, Donna Camp, Dorothy Caskanette, Clare Churchward, Debbie Dowling, Karl Edmison, Norma Farrish, Patricia Grikinis, Nirmala Jilka, Lloyd Kitchen, Gregg Lloyd, Harry Lloyd, Kim Mannen, Ada Near, Paul Near, and Larry Wilson.

Saskatoon: Helen Faulkner, Aleta Jorgenson, Anita Messaros, Barb Money, Bernie Rousell, and Terry Wishlow.

Winnipeg: David Rich and Larry Gobeil

EDMONTON WAS IN THE MIDST of a real estate boom in 1911 when founders Charles A. Graham, Alexander C. Rutherford, and Alfred E. Jackson tied the future of their company to the future of Edmonton, and of Alberta, by providing good-quality clothing made by working women for working men building the West. Three simple but bold words reflected the origin and the foundation of the company — Great, Western, Garment.

This is a story of management and labour working collaboratively towards a common goal, of being one of the first garment manufacturing companies to introduce the eight-hour day and forty-four-hour week, a company so proud of its working conditions in the early years that it published pictures of the factory in advertisements targeted to other unionized workers, farmers, and labourers.

It is a story of innovation and quality, of Snobak pre-shrunk denim, developed by GWG at Canadian Cottons in Cornwall, Ontario, and Scrubbies, the original pre-washed jeans, invented in Edmonton. It is a story of efforts to appeal to a younger, not necessarily western, market through Peace Jeans and George (and the less familiar Grace) W. Groovey. It is a story of the waves of immigration to Edmonton and their integration into their new community, and of the company's efforts to accommodate their experience. Ultimately, it is a story of globalization and the struggle to survive and compete in Canada when most multinational garment manufacturing companies moved offshore.

An Edmonton Company

Alberta is known throughout Canada for its agricultural and resource-based economy. In the early twentieth century, Montreal, Toronto, and Winnipeg were all more significant garment manufacturing centres than either Edmonton or Calgary, but the Great Western Garment Company—Canada's largest work clothing manufacturing company — was distinctly Albertan. The initials "GWG" were first a brand of Edmonton's Great Western Garment Company, but soon became synonymous with the company itself. The GWG story is one of national significance, yet today it is little known or appreciated in Edmonton, let alone nationally.

Garment unions in early twentieth-century Montreal, Toronto, and Winnipeg met much more resistance from manufacturers than did the union at the Great Western Garment Company. Eastern unions were more confrontational in their approach to management and held frequent work stoppages. Academic attention has rightly focused on sweatshops, homework, and labour disputes, whereas the story of the Great Western Garment Company is, generally, a much more positive story.

While garment manufacturing can be a very volatile industry, easy to enter with relatively low overhead,

Great Western Garment took a different approach. Unlike the dozens of smaller, often family firms, of the eastern cities, which required little commitment or investment, GWG thought big from the outset. The fact that there were fewer companies, and fewer potential workers in Alberta, encouraged employers to offer better working conditions and discouraged sweatshops and outsourcing.

In the early years, Great Western Garment could succeed far from the style centre in New York because the company produced men's workwear. The company manufactured the same lines year after year, with standardized cut and styling, requiring less skilled labour to produce than women's fashionable clothing. The market for ready-made clothing was primarily men, as was the population of Western Canada.

At the time, mass manufacture of women's clothing lagged behind menswear. Most women living in Edmonton would have used local dressmakers or made their own clothing inspired by illustrations in catalogues and magazines and patterns, whereas menswear was usually produced in larger, machine-oriented plants.

Winnipeg's dominance as the regional metropolis for Western Canada declined after the opening of the Panama Canal in 1914. International goods and resources began to be shipped by sea from Vancouver rather than through Winnipeg by rail. In 1920, Vancouver surpassed Winnipeg as Canada's third-largest city. However, even though Winnipeg's firms were predominantly small family operations, Winnipeg remained the yardstick against which Alberta garment manufacturers measured their success. Through efficiencies of scale and good management, Great Western Garment dominated the workwear industry.

Several factors contributed to the Great Western Garment Company's early success, including high-quality products, innovation, flexibility, cooperation between the union and management, Western boosterism, and federal government policies. By the beginning of World War II, the *Edmonton Journal* claimed that Great Western Garment was the largest workwear manufacturing company in the British Empire.

Great Western Garment was a major supplier of military and prisoner-of-war uniforms during both world wars. After World War II, GWG expanded its product lines beyond men's and boys' workwear, and a very limited range of ladies' workwear and sportswear, into casual clothing for the whole family. Its marketing and distribution network grew from Western Canada to include the entire country.

Beginning in the mid-1960s, Great Western Garment bought existing factories in Winnipeg, Manitoba, and in Brantford, Ontario, and in 1973 built a new factory in Saskatoon, Saskatchewan. Levi Strauss bought the majority of shares of GWG in 1961, the remainder in 1972, and opened its own factories in Cornwall and Stoney Creek, Ontario.

Although Levi Strauss owned GWG, the two companies operated independently until 1982, when Levi Strauss and GWG began to operate under the Great Northern Apparel banner. Within a few years, Levi Strauss began to absorb GWG into its corporate structure. In March 2004, when Levi Strauss ended its long manufacturing history in North America to contract all manufacturing offshore, the last Levi's plant closed was in Edmonton, where 488 workers were laid off.

After nearly one hundred years, the GWG brand is no longer produced in Edmonton. Instead, GWG jeans are now imported from Bangladesh and other countries. Ultimately, the closure of the Edmonton factory was symptomatic of the loss of so many garment manufacturing companies in Canada, but it was a huge loss to the city and the country. It was the end of an era.

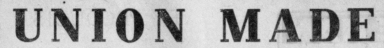

UNION MADE

IS AN IMPORTANT PART OF OUR TRADE MARK

UNION MADE

It is a guarantee that we are co-operating with union labor in an effort to attain the highest results for all concerned in our industry.

All workers who use OVERALLS, PANTS or SHIRTS help the cause

by demanding  Brand whenever they buy.

UNION MADE

"THEY WEAR LONGER BECAUSE THEY'RE MADE STRONGER"

THE GREAT WESTERN GARMENT CO. LTD.
—EDMONTON—

Union Made

In 1911 Great Western Garment registered its trademark interlocking initials with wings and a red dot, and the words "Union Made." Here GWG emphasized the words "Union Made" and omitted the dot. The UGWA provided a separate union made label that indicates unionized workers produced the garments under a negotiated agreement, as opposed to manufacture through outsourcing or in a sweatshop. During negotiations, the union could withhold the use of the label until they reached an agreement with management. In the early twentieth century, the union label was very important to workers in other unionized firms and to people concerned about fair trade. *Alberta Labor News*, October 16, 1920. PAA, PR1970.0394

1911-1929

CHAPTER ONE

IN 1911 EDMONTON'S ECONOMY was booming. Real estate values were high: many new shops, businesses, and industries such as confectionery, meat packing, and brewing were established; new houses were built. The Great Western Garment Company (GWG) was the first garment manufacturing company to be established in Edmonton, on January 30, 1911, during this optimistic period.

Great Western Garment was founded by President Alfred E. Jackson (former city councillor and co-owner of the Alberta Hotel), Vice-President Alexander C. Rutherford (solicitor and former premier), and Manager Charles A. Graham (former buyer and salesman with the dry goods branch of the Revillon firm). Jackson and Rutherford, along with fifteen other investors, provided the lion's share of the initial $75,000 capital required, while Graham provided industry experience. The founders shared a strong belief in the promising future of the young city. They had an eye on the need to supply a growing workforce with functional, hard-wearing clothing, suitable for the climate.

Local 120, United Garment Workers of America Charter, 1911

Workers founded the United Garment Workers of America (UGWA) in New York City in 1891 and affiliated with the American Federation of Labor (AFL). In 1914 a large group of dissatisfied members broke away from the conservative UGWA to form the Amalgamated Clothing Workers of America (ACWA). The ACWA also focused on the men's and boys' clothing industry. Local 120, like most other work clothing locals, remained a part of UGWA. In Edmonton, the union was affiliated with both the Edmonton Trades and Labour Council (ETLC), and, after it was established in 1912, the Alberta Federation of Labour (AFL). Local 120 Collection. PAA

Unionization

About two months later, on April 3, 1911, the United Garment Workers of America (UGWA) chartered Local 120 with just seven workers, the minimum required. Unionization may have been initiated by management as a form of "company union," a collaborative union with a particularly close relationship to the company. Local 120 was one of few UGWA locals in Western Canada. Most of UGWA's more than three thousand Canadian members at the time lived in Montreal or Toronto and had more access to the headquarters in New York. Great Western Garment unionized under UGWA during the period in which there was a growing divide between conservative members of the union and the more radical faction that in 1914 broke away to form the Amalgamated Clothing Workers of America.

Great Western Garment workers unionized in part in response to the Triangle Shirtwaist Factory fire in New York City on March 25, 1911—the worst disaster in the city's history prior to 9/11—in which 146 of 500 employees, primarily young women, died. Management intentionally kept the emergency doors locked to prevent workers from going out onto the fire escape. The front page of Edmonton's *Evening Journal*, March 28, 1911, reported the tragedy. Workers and management alike were aware of the potential dangers of sweatshops.

Certainly, management supported unionization because they wanted to use union labels on their products in order to promote sales to other unionized workers in industries such as mining and railways. In labour publications Great Western Garment made a direct appeal to labour to "help the cause" by buying goods from a company that was "co-operating with labor in an effort to attain the highest results for all concerned." Similarly, other unions appealed to GWG workers to purchase their products and services or provide financial and moral support—to join the picket line and not to cross the picket line—during a strike.

The *Edmonton Journal*, November 28, 1914, noted Great Western Garment's rejection of sweatshop conditions: "they have made it impossible for a sweatshop ever to be established in this line in Edmonton. They pay the union scale of wages and keep expert help in all departments."

The factory's assembly line system was initially fairly basic. In a small factory with few specialized machines, it is impossible to break production down into very many steps. Cutters and their apprentices spread the fabric and piled twenty to sixty layers (depending upon the weight of the fabric) to be cut at once. Max Bedard, who started work as a bundle boy in 1916, remembered that bundle boys — sometimes as young as fourteen — separated the cut pieces and divided them up, matching fronts to backs for example. They bundled enough pieces to make twenty or thirty garments, tagged them, and carried them to the seamstresses for sewing.

Examiners checked completed garments for quality control and sent them back to the operators for repairs if there were any problems, such as loose buttons or dangling threads. The company modified the piecework system through the years. Initially, seamstresses made entire garments, then production was divided into several operations —pants, for example, included inseams, side seams, waistbands, buttons, and later divided further and further.

The company quickly became a significant employer of women in Edmonton. According to company records, Great Western Garment's workforce increased from the initial seven to more than one hundred workers (mostly women) and from four to twelve sales staff (men) in its first year of operation. In 1914 the plant took over the building next door and doubled its space at 10438 Namayo Street (renamed 97 Street) to accommodate its expanding workforce of 150 operators. Although the vast majority of union members were women, most of its early leaders were men. The executive always included people working in a variety of jobs within the plant, cutters and mechanics, as well as operators.

The Union Label

The union label is evidence that unionized workers produced goods under a negotiated agreement between labour and management. In the garment industry, it is a guarantee that the clothes were not outsourced or produced in a sweatshop. In the first half of the twentieth century, the union label was very important. During difficult negotiations, UGWA's strategy was not to threaten strike action but to with-hold the use of the label until they reached an agreement with management. By 1950 the label had lost some of its significance and UGWA instructed locals to boost the union label.
Local 120 Collection. PAA

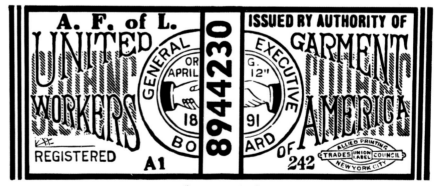

MARKETING TO LABOUR

When the Great Western Garment Company organized under the United Garment Workers of America (UGWA) in April 1911, management supported unionization because the company wanted to use union labels on its products, to promote sales to other unionized workers. In turn, GWG's workers were encouraged to patronize particular businesses that used unionized labour.

Great Western Garment advertised its excellent working conditions, and ran a series of ads appealing to workers in Western Canada, linking garment manufacturing to other significant industries.

Its early ads targeted farmers, miners, lumbermen, railwaymen, and mechanics, many of whom would have been unionized. Advertisements often featured clothing being worn by workers in specific occupations, pointing out the features that were required for each job. For example, painters and carpenters wore white overalls with reinforced knees and pockets and loops for rulers, tools, and brushes.

"Union Made is an important part of our trade mark," GWG advertised in the *Alberta Labor News*, 1921. "It is a guarantee that we are co-operating with union labor in an effort to attain the highest results for all concerned in our industry. All workers who use overall, pants or shirts help the cause by demanding GWG Brand whenever they buy."

Great Western Garment appealed to non-unionized workers as well. Advertisements showed men working in a variety of occupations: highway construction, fishing, dairy farming, ranching, construction, oil, and grain farming. The message was that no matter what your occupation, there was a GWG work shirt for you.

When GWG expanded throughout Canada in the 1950s and early 1960s, the company marketed to a broad range of workers, not just to those in Western Canadian occupations. The emphasis was on quality, fit, and durability, the "longer wear and perfect fit that Canadians in every walk of life have come to know and appreciate," rather than on the union.

GWG work pants, c. 1915.
Lucie Heins, RAM, H08.78.1

Carpenters' overalls, c. 1965.
Lucie Heins, RAM, H08.17.84

Farm and Ranch Review, April 21, 1919.
Reynolds-Alberta Museum

Vitality

Canada's greatest National asset is the inherent vitality of Her glorious MANHOOD.

The Manhood of Western Canada is one vast Industrial Army in which is enrolled over 80 per cent. of the Country's adult male population.

An army of "Uniformed" workers—farmers, miners, lumbermen, railwaymen, mechanics.

Vitality and efficiency require special clothing for the worker adapted to his individual employment—comfort, durability and perfect freedom of arm, leg and body movement are his ideals realized in G.W.G. garments.

Hence the demand for these garments which now calls for factory production at the rate of $2,000,000 a year.

The present offering of shares in the Great Western Garment Company constitutes an investment opportunity carrying the highest banking and commercial endorsement and combining safety of principal with the assurance of increasing yield and enhancement of value.

8% First Preference Shares

(Carrying a bonus of $25 per share, par value, of fully paid Second Preference Stock)

$100 PER SHARE, PAR

Prospectus upon application.

Great Western Garment Co. Ltd.
EDMONTON

Alberta Labor News, October 22, 1921.
PAA, PR1970.0394

Farm and Ranch Review, June 5, 1920.
Reynolds-Alberta Museum

23

The Garment District

The *Henderson's Directories* trace the development of a garment manufacturing district along Namayo Street from Jasper to Griesbach (now 105 Avenue) near the railway line. Independent dressmakers, milliners, tailors, shoemakers, furriers, tent makers, and others working in related businesses such as dry cleaning and retail clothing located their businesses in this district. LaFlèche Bros. tailoring moved to Jasper Avenue following the amalgamation of Edmonton and Strathcona in 1912. In addition to custom-made and ready-to-wear suits, the forty workers at LaFlèche Bros. manufactured uniforms for the city's street railway and fire department workers. Ramsey's department store established Emery Manufacturing, a ladies wear factory, at the corner of Namayo and Griesbach in January 1913, where eighty operators manufactured ladies' blouses, dresses, and skirts.

Two competing overall and pant manufacturers were established a few years later. Courtney Manufacturing, a shirt, blouse, and overall manufacturer, was at 10349-97 Street from 1920 to 1921, then moved to 9609-103A Avenue, and finally to 10607-97 Street where it operated as a wholesaler from 1924 to 1932. A few blocks away, Northwestern Manufacturing was at 10261-108 Street from 1922 to 1929, and as a clothing wholesaler, from 1930 to 1932 at 10185-107 Street. The firm employed more than seventy-five people making shirts, blouses, pants, and overalls.

Reynolds Manufacturing, which is still producing clothing in Edmonton today, was established in 1928 at 9832-113 Street, in the basement of the home of Harold N. Reynolds, former managing chef in the GWG cafeteria.

There were also a number of short-lived concerns established in this area in the 1910s and 1920s: James B. McCormack, hosiery manufacturer (1912-1913), Kays Overall Manufacturers (1914-1919), the Edmonton Knitting Company (1919-1927), Grace Lingerie Manufacturing Co., Economy Commercial Co. Ltd., and the Alberta Garment Manufacturers Ltd. (1929).

Former workers described how they would often move between businesses in the early years, making overalls one week and tents the next, depending upon where there were employment opportunities. Because of this, working conditions and salaries were comparable.

The population of Edmonton more than doubled between 1911 and 1913, through the amalgamation of Edmonton and Strathcona and land speculation, growing from 31,064 to 67,243. However, few jobs were available to Canadian women before World War II. Many employers would not retain married women because employers expected women to stay at home, look after their husbands, and raise children. They forced women to resign when they married. Single women also had few legitimate employment opportunities.

Yet it was a fallacy that women's work was temporary, just a stop-gap between finishing school and marrying and having children. Many women needed to work to support their families because their husbands were unable or unwilling to do so. Women working in garment manufacturing were able to earn considerably more than those working in other traditionally female occupations such as the service industry, where the minimum wage was usually the maximum wage they could expect.

In the early years, workers at the Great Western Garment plant were primarily English-speaking—immigrants from the United Kingdom and the United States and migrants from Eastern Canada.

The first large groups of immigrants to come to Alberta in the late nineteenth and early twentieth centuries came to homestead and settle on the Prairies rather than to populate cities. With the restriction of immigration immediately

Great Western Garment Factory, 1911-1917

From 1911 to 1917, the GWG factory was in a 1,540-square metre, $150,000 building on the northeast corner of 105 Avenue and 97 Street. McDermid Studios published this photograph in 1914 as part of a collage of local industries featured in *Edmonton: Alberta's Capital City*, a booklet promoting Edmonton as a prosperous young city. As the workforce increased, the company expanded into the space next door.

Photograph by Frederick Glen McDermid. COEA, A94-18

Great Western Garment Cutting Room, 1913
August Frasch took this interior photograph of the cutting room after GWG moved the sewing room to the second floor. Here a number of men can be seen spreading fabric and cutting, using both mechanical cutters and large cutting shears. Cutters were able to cut twenty to sixty layers of fabric at once, depending upon the thickness of the fabric. Photograph by August B. Frasch. PAA, B1139

before, during, and after World War I, integration of non-English-speaking immigrants into the factory was later at GWG than it had been in Eastern American and Canadian firms. Edmonton did not have a significant population of European Jews like those whose socialist vision impacted the union movement in Montreal, Toronto, and Winnipeg. Like UGWA generally, the workforce at GWG was, at first, largely made up of established North American workers.

"Made in the West for the West"
Most local manufacturers produced only for local consumption. Although GWG's original market was local, the company had a more regional outlook and larger ambition. Great Western Garment limited sales to the western provinces: British Columbia, Alberta, and Saskatchewan, and they introduced the slogan "Made in the West for the West." The sales force grew to sixteen in 1916. GWG provided salesmen with company cars to visit rural districts; salesmen took the train as new areas were opened up.

To avoid competing with the more established garment manufacturers in Winnipeg, GWG did not initially sell garments in Manitoba. Although Winnipeg had more garment manufacturing companies than did Edmonton, they were primarily family-run operations employing only a handful of workers who continued to make clothing one garment at a time.

Great Western Garment built upon the relationship between manufacturing and agriculture. The company stated in the *Farm and Ranch Review*, February 5, 1918, that its goal was: "to take up the slack in the centres of population, where the boys and girls who do not desire

Great Western Garment Interior, 1911

This interior photograph provides insight into working conditions in the first factory, a long, narrow building, with cutting and sewing taking place in the same room. It shows that from the beginning, GWG divided labour along gender lines. There are sixteen women sewing at machines facing one another. The woman and man in the foreground are working on specialized machines. The man in the background, possibly the cutter, is standing beside stacks of cut pant pieces. There is little debris on the floor. Bare bulbs hanging from the ceiling supplement the natural light from the windows. GA, NC-6-62221

Great Western Garment Paper Puzzle, c. 1916

GWG produced this unique paper puzzle that folds into a pair of pants and also serves as a poster with humorous illustrations of GWG shirts and overalls. The drawings provide details about quality in fit and construction and feature mechanics, farmers, and miners all happily wearing GWGs. GWG offered a fifty-dollar reward — a huge sum of money at the time — to the person submitting the best folded design of a shirt. Was it ever claimed? The reverse side of the puzzle was printed to look like denim with markings for the fly, pockets, and suspender buttons to provide a guide to folding the pants.

Bulman Bros. Ltd., Lithd. Winnipeg, Private Collection

Great Western Garment Sewing Room, 1916

The sewing room on the second floor has skylights to improve the lighting available for the women here sewing striped overalls. By this time, the workforce had expanded to more than 150 operators crowded in long rows of machines side by side. This was a posed photograph. However, you can see that GWG had already addressed safety issues later raised in the Factories Act of 1917, such as adequate light, buckets of water to fight fire, and women's hair pulled back to prevent getting caught in machinery.
Photograph by Byron-May Co. NC-6-66520

to follow agriculture may go, to find satisfactory and profitable employment not too far from the old home and where we can develop a ready market for our farm products."

In 1915 Great Western Garment began to fill wartime contracts. The *Edmonton Journal* reported that GWG manufactured three thousand shirts for the Canadian government and twenty thousand pairs of British Army service trousers (a $70,000 contract), with a promise of more wartime contracts to follow. The union negotiated time and a half for the overtime necessary to meet wartime demands.

Military contracts provided a buffer for the seasonal purchases (and therefore production) of work clothes. As machinist Max Bedard remembered, "If the farmers didn't get rain in June we used to get a couple of months holiday in the summer." C.A. Graham became manager in 1916 and continued to expand the company with the cooperation of labour. As the company expanded, so did its ability to order materials in quantity, buy on better terms, receive prompt delivery, and reduce the per unit cost to produce goods.

Working Conditions

The provincial government introduced an Act for the Protection of Persons Employed in Factories, Shops and Office Buildings (the Factories Act) in 1917 to protect workers in Alberta. Although similar in many respects to legislation in other provinces, Alberta was the first province to introduce the principle of minimum wage. The act legislated against juvenile labour, but according to former workers who started work at the age of fourteen, in the years immediately following the introduction of the Factories Act, a boy could "state his age and if he had the height" the employer did not question him.

The act also governed the physical environment required in factories, construction and layout, safety, cleanliness, and fire prevention. Alongside local and provincial labour organizations, Local 120 lobbied to improve labour legislation. The company demonstrated through advertisements in labour and agricultural publications of the period that its working conditions were better than those required by the government through its proposed legislation.

From 1917 to 1953, the factory was located at the corner of 97 Street and 103 Avenue. Constructed as a department store in 1911, the building was converted for use as a factory. GWG said that the plant was considered "one of the finest on the continent from the standpoint of the worker."

Great Western Garment's sewing machine operators worked fewer hours than did other workers in Alberta. Local 120 was—if not the first—one of the first garment manufacturing unions in North America to negotiate the eight-hour day and forty-four-hour week. Labour activist and later mayor Elmer E. Roper noted in provincial labour legislation debates in 1927 that GWG had been "the first on the continent to establish the eight-hour day and the forty-four hour week." However, when the Amalgamated Clothing Workers (ACWA) signed an agreement with Toronto manufacturers on March 22, 1917, granting the forty-four-hour week, it claimed that the ACWA was the first to establish a real eight-hour day. Great Western Garment's letterhead in 1917 stated, "Where the eight hour day and fair wages prevail."

The eight-hour day was a significant breakthrough. The Edmonton Trades and Labour Council (ETLC) and the Alberta Federation of Labour (AFL) continued to lobby the provincial government to legislate an eight-hour day and forty-hour week for workers throughout the province through the 1920s. The provincial government was still debating about limiting working hours to nine per day and establishing a forty-eight-hour week in 1926.

Appeal to Labour

In 1920 Great Western Garment ran advertisements in labour and farming publications showing "contented" workers, satisfactory working conditions, and the subsidized cafeteria. They promote the positive relationship between management and labour. The work pants department appears clean, with sunlight streaming in the windows, and overhead lighting. Inset photographs compare the modern sewing room to the first workroom: workers appear less crowded and fire extinguishers replace water buckets. Photograph by Frederick Glen McDermid. GA, NC6-3269

GIRLS WANTED

To work under the most sanitary and wholesome conditions and working shorter hours than any other factory in this trade in Canada

UNION MADE

REGISTERED TRADE MARK

THESE ARE THE PRODUCTS OF THE MOST CAPABLE ORGANIZATION OF WOMEN IN WESTERN CANADA:

Men's and Boys' Overalls   Men's and Boys' Shirts
Men's Pants and Combination Overalls

HERE IS OUR PROPOSITION TO YOU:

If you are over seventeen and possessed of good health, we will give you steady employment, paying you on the piece-work basis, many girls in our factory earning $16.00 to $24.00 per week.

If you have not had experience we will pay you $9.00 per week while learning. Some girls pass out of this

class in two weeks; some in four. We employ instructors to assist you in every possible way, as it is to our interest as much as yours that you develop this useful art as quickly as possible.

Apply now in person at our factory on 97th street, and do not delay, for we expect in a few days to have every machine filled. Ask for Mr. Sutcliffe.

The Great Western Garment Co.

LIMITED

97th Street, Edmonton, Alberta

Girls Wanted

When Great Western Garment moved to the new factory, the company expanded its workforce. This advertisement ran for weeks in the *Edmonton Free Press* and *Alberta Labor News*. GWG invited girls over the age of seventeen to apply, and emphasized the good working conditions in the plant, the relatively high rates earned on piecework, and the relatively short hours of work compared to other garment manufacturing companies. GWG paid women nine dollars a week while in training. They could earn sixteen dollars to twenty-four dollars a week once they became proficient. Good health was the only requirement.

Edmonton Free Press, October 18, 1919, p. 3.
PAA, PR1970.0394

OPPOSITE: **Great Western Garment Factory, 1917-1953**
For thirty-six years, the Great Western Garment factory was on the northeast corner of 97 Street and 103 Avenue, at 10305-97 Street. Built in 1911 by Alexander Livingstone, owner of the Caledonian Department Store, the three-storey building was a good example of the Edwardian Commercial style, functional yet decorative. Originally, the second-floor windows had segmental arched heads, the third-storey windows were rectilinear and filled the structural bays, pilasters separated the windows, and a balustrade rose above the cornice. McDermid Studios took this photograph in November 1917, shortly after GWG moved into the building. Photograph by Frederick Glen McDermid. GA NC6-2913

Concerning a Neighbor of Yours

Great Industries Of Our Great West

No. 1---Dairying:

WESTERN Canada dairy-farmers are now producing milk at the rate of two million six hundred thousand quarts a day—a quantity as large as the entire daily consumption of Greater New York City, whose population equals that of the whole of Canada.

One million two hundred thousand milch cows, comprising many of the world's finest herds, valued at seventy-five million dollars, furnish the milk supply each year for twenty-five million dollars worth of dairy products, including twelve million dollars worth of butter, and add over fifty million dollars annually to our agricultural revenues. From Liverpool to Yokohama Western Canada butter and cheese commands the primacy of the world's markets on quality.

The dairyman's operations, from the farm to the finished factory product, are conducted with the utmost regard for scientific considerations, and the vast army of over one hundred thousand discriminating men and boys engaged in the production and manufacture of milk regard The Great Western Garment Company as a neighbor industry which understands and provides their particular requirements in work-clothing— besides helping them to make Western Canada a land of opportunity created by the prosperity of her industries.

UNION MADE

Sold Everywhere by Merchants whose Purchasing Power Permits them to Buy the Best

However, the piecework system put pressure on women to work very quickly and to work additional time to complete more pieces, clean their machines, or do repairs for which they were not paid. Piecework price lists were set through negotiations between the union and management. In some ways, Local 120 had a closer relationship to the Edmonton Trades and Labour Council than it did to UGWA, as representatives from Toronto or New York rarely came to Edmonton to assist in contract negotiations. If necessary, the ETLC occasionally supported the union's position.

Operators who worked faster earned more than minimum wage, in some cases significantly more. In the early years, the union restricted the number of operations GWG could ask a woman to do to a maximum of three, as they earned more money with more practice on fewer operations. A number of operators commented that they were sorry to move from the assembly line, where they earned piecework rates, to a job that paid by the hour, such as inspecting, because they would earn less money on the weekly rate.

Disputes between workers and the company were minor and usually easily resolved. Complaints often related to time lost waiting for bundle boys or girls to bring work, cleaning and maintaining machines, replacing broken needles or thread, or waiting for a mechanic to repair a machine.

Apprentice mechanics and cutters asked the union to intervene to allow them to learn the trade and accordingly earn higher wages. Operators whose pay dropped when moved to a different machine or operation sometimes initiated a grievance. The union helped operators move to higher-paying

Great Industries

Great Western Garment aligned the company with other profitable western industries in a series of advertisements directed towards men working in specific industries such as dairy farming, mining, and railways. The ads equated the challenges and successes of other industries with those of GWG, and tied the future of these industries to the future of GWG and of the West. *Farmer's Advocate and Home Journal,* January 25, 1924. Reynolds-Alberta Museum

machines or to learn more skilled work. It also argued on behalf of workers who were wrongfully dismissed or dismissed without severance.

"They Wear Longer Because They're Made Stronger"

In 1918 Great Western Garment introduced the slogan "They wear longer because they're made stronger," which was featured in GWG advertisements for many years. Great Western Garment issued a series of comical ads in publications like the *Farm and Ranch Review* and the *Farmer's Advocate and Home Journal,* demonstrating the strength of its garments and their appropriateness for various tasks.

Great Western Garment established a reputation for quality goods suitable for the hard work of farmers, coal miners, railway workers, and others developing the West. The company even guaranteed its products, saying: "Every garment bearing the G.W.G. Label is guaranteed to give full satisfaction to the wearer in fit, workmanship and quality, and to obtain his satisfaction, should the garment prove defective, simply satisfy the merchant from whom purchased; he is authorized by us to replace it."

By 1919 GWG employed 375 workers. Although Local 120 made significant inroads to benefit its own members and worked with the provincial government to improve labour legislation, the union was not inclined to get involved in larger labour disputes or radical unrest. Local 120 demonstrated its conservatism when it was one of only four unions in Edmonton to vote not to strike in support of the Winnipeg General Strike.

Along with the increase in the factory's square metres and the size of its workforce, GWG's sales increased dramatically in its first decade of operation, from $48,000 in 1911 to $1.5 million in 1920, according to an advertisement in the *Alberta Labor News,* April 9, 1921, offering shares in the company. C.A. Graham became president in 1920. His co-founders A.E. Jackson and A.C. Rutherford, and Rutherford's son Cecil, sold their shares the following year. Through these advertisements, and as Alberta's Consumer and Corporate Affairs recorded, GWG increased its capital base from $125,000 to $750,000. At the same time, falling grain prices, real estate and railway speculation led to an economic recession in the province. The company emphasized its stability in good economic times and in bad because, unlike fashionable clothing, there would always be a demand for workwear.

Great Western Garment continued to expand through diversification. GWG made a variety of different types of clothing in addition to workwear. Some of the more successful lines introduced in the 1920s include black pants, referred to as "Sunday pants for the farmers," and mackinaw jackets. Mackinaw is a Canadian word for short coats made of thick woollen cloth, often plaid and with a sheepskin collar. However, mackinaws were very difficult to sew as the cloth was heavy and filled the air with lint. One former employee noted that working in the mackinaw department during this period exacerbated the respiratory problems she had endured since childhood. GWG also began to work with Alberta wool producers to develop local woollen mills, producing yarn and fabric—called west wool—adapted to western climatic conditions. By 1927 Great Western Garment produced seventeen thousand garments annually.

Minimum Wage

In 1922 the Alberta government introduced an Act to Provide a Minimum Wage for Women. There were two divisions within manufacturing: needle trades and other industries. Working women were often exploited, underpaid, and overworked, by manufacturers. Similarly, they were often

Investment Opportunity

In 1921 the company offered workers the opportunity to buy shares through advertisements such as this one in the *Alberta Labor News*. Great Western Garment raised more than enough capital to buy out founders A. E. Jackson and A.C. Rutherford and increased loyalty within the labour community at the same time. The inset image of a man lifting the weight of another holding a pair of GWGs was one of a series of advertisements used at the time to demonstrate the strength of GWG clothing and the truth in the slogan, "They wear longer because they're made stronger."

Alberta Labor News, April 9, 1921, p. 7.
PAA, PR1970.0394

A Commodity as Staple as the Agriculture of Western Canada

The wise investor will place his money in an industry where returns will be sure in hard times. Almost any business can earn a profit for a while, or during an era of prosperity, but it is when hard times come that interest on our investments is needed most.

Before investing, it is well to ask whether there is a permanent demand for the product of the industry. Many factories making specialties or fashionable goods do well for a time but find themselves out of business because of a change in fashion, or because the market for the specialty is filled and there are no repeat orders. Such businesses have no chance to build up an army of loyal customers, who keep coming back regularly for new supplies.

No such danger exists in the business of making workingmen's clothing. Such staple clothing must be replaced at frequent intervals and a company that establishes a reputation for satisfactory goods will enjoy the regular patronage of pleased customers.

The Great Western Garment Company Limited, has succeeded in placing itself in the leading position for the manufacture and sale of workingmen's clothing in Western Canada. In ten years their sales have increased from $48,000 in 1911 to $1,500,000 in 1920.

The reason for this success is that the business was founded and is managed by western men who konw the needs of the country because they live in it.

An opportunity to invest in this established Western industry is now open to you. Owing to the growing demand for their products, the Company is increasing its capital, and a block of first preference shares is now offered at $100.00 per share, with a bonus of 25% in Participating Second Preference Shares.

SELLING AGENTS

GWG
UNION MADE
REGISTERED TRADE MARK

OVERALLS

"They wear longer because they're made stronger"

THE GREAT WESTERN GARMENT COMPANY, LTD
EDMONTON ALBERTA

North West Securities Corporation, Limited

EDMONTON, ALBERTA   PHONE 5376

Kindly permit us to send a man to you who will explain the details without obligation on your part.
Ring 5376.

Blue Diamond Overalls

In 1921 Great Western Garment introduced Blue Diamond overalls designed specifically for railway workers. This advertisement underlines the collaboration between the railway workers and GWG in the development of the overalls. A committee of railway workers was involved in their design and testing, and a railway local provided the name. Innovations include particularly wide suspenders, a high back, and pocket features that prevent objects from falling out. In 1924 GWG ran a series of advertisements targeting workers in specific industries in Alberta, including railway workers.

Alberta Labor News, March 8, 1921
PAA, PR1970.0394

The G.W.G. "Blue Diamond" High Back Overall

You know how Railroad men are particular about their overalls—how they insist upon a long roomy garment that gives the utmost freedom of action. The "Blue Diamond" High Back Overall is the finally approved garment which the railroad men declared to be perfect in every way. They are the most critical of all overall users, and with their approval it may be confidently assumed that there is nothing better than the G.W.G. "Blue Diamond."

The railroad men of the West were continually applying to us to construct an overall suited to their particular use. We finally agreed to take a co-operative interest with them, and a committee of railroad men, in conjunction with our de-

The name selected, "Blue Diamond," was suggested by Local No. 715, B. of L., at Saskatoon. The Overall will carry a blue Diamond shaped label on the diamond-shaped space where the suspenders cross—the "Blue" denoting the color of the overall and the "Diamond" indicating its superior quality.

The denim in the "Blue Diamond" is an extra heavy weight and a specially close woven cloth. It is as unshrinkable as any denim can be made, and all parts of the garment are designed to carry extra fullness of cloth where necessary to guard against shrinking.

The back reaches up higher, taking more cloth than almost any other overall, serving the double purpose of protecting the kidneys against cold or wind, and at the same time covering more of the clothing.

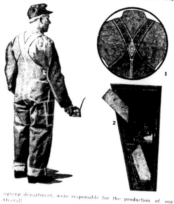

SOME SPECIAL FEATURES

All the special features are protected by Canadian Patents held by this Company for your protection.

(1) Wide Suspenders crossed high up, giving extra protection to the back and kidneys. No seams or buttons attaching suspenders to the garment. (Look for the Blue Diamond.)

(2) Double Rule Pocket with reinforced lining and Patented Lock. Try to shake a rule or pair of pliers out of this pocket. **This test should be featured—it's a most convincing one, and it really demonstrates the wonderful safety device better than any words.**

(3) Put a Watch in the Bib Pocket. Let it go to the bottom of the pocket. Turn the overall upside down. Shake it, whirl it around your head. The watch goes under the extra sewed-in flap. It can't get out until you take it out.

(4) Note the extra sewed-in flaps in the front safety pockets. Your money, knife, etc., will not drop out of these pockets, no matter in what position you may be.

The suspenders are extra wide and extra strong, being a continuation of the back itself. They cross high up on the back, and consequently will not easily come off the shoulders. The suspenders are finished with heavy brass loops and slides, while all buttons are heavy oxidized brass.

Pockets and inside bands are made from strong heavy drill. Every point of strain is doubly reinforced by special tacking, and the outside seams are felled and double stitched.

signing department, were responsible for the production of our new high back Overall

When the design was finally decided upon we submitted samples to the various railwaymen's locals throughout the West for their approval, and for a special name to distinguish it as the particular Overall given official approval by railroad men themselves.

The general comfort of the "Blue Diamond" is one of its finest features---it's very big, it is as carefully designed as though it were a hand-tailored suit. The material in this garment is worthy of special note, as its quality is decidedly better than any other we have seen, and of some interest to you is the fact that we are going to continue to sell this garment at exactly the same price, with all these added features, as is being asked for ordinary overalls. Not one cent extra for "Blue Diamond" features. Perhaps, of importance to you is the fact this overall is made in Edmonton.

Edmonton Firm Believes in Using Edmonton-Made Products

The above illustrations are reduced reproductions of a set of five hanger cards in four colors that are just completed for the Great Western Garment Company, Ltd. The order comprises 10,000 cards, 13x17 inches, and they are reproduced in what is known, technically, as the four color process. This is the largest exclusive color job of any consequence ever placed in the city of Edmonton.

It might be interesting to note that the G.W.G. overalls have the largest sale, in Western Canada, of any overalls, and the extensive and aggressive advertising campaign promoted by the Great Western Garment Company, Ltd., and the color printing was done by Esdale Press, Ltd. Both are Edmonton firms.

The color drawings and color plates are the work of the McDermid Engraving Company, Ltd., and the color printing was done by Esdale Press, Ltd. Both are Edmonton firms.

The Great Western Garment Company are to be complimented for their confidence in local firms and their loyalty to Edmonton-made products in placing this large order locally instead of sending it East.

Edmonton Made Products

In the 1910s and 1920s, a recurring theme in the Great Western Garment Company's advertisements was the importance of supporting local industry. GWG demonstrated its support of other Edmonton-based companies, in this case the McDermid Engraving Company and Esdale Press Ltd. The *Edmonton Bulletin* led a campaign, called Patronize Local Industry, that featured GWG and other local companies. *Alberta Labor News*, January 22, 1921, p. 4. PAA, PR1970.0394

GWG Delegates at the Alberta Federation of Labour Annual Convention, 1925
Lillian Morris, third from the left in the front row, was one of GWG's delegates—and one of only three
women—who attended the Alberta Federation of Labour convention in 1925. Morris began working at GWG
in 1915 after losing her job with the City of Edmonton when she got married. She became very involved in the
union and represented employees on the Minimum Wage Board for ten years, from 1924 to 1934. Morris always
tried to improve the situation for working women, but it was a challenge to balance the interests of employers
and employees on the board. Courtesy of Lillian Morris

neglected by male-dominated unions — even in female-dominated companies. That was not the case at Great Western Garment where women were active within the union, and the union was listened to provincially. In the early years, Local 120's delegates were among the few women participating in the labour movement locally and provincially.

Local 120 influenced the hours, wages, and working conditions of other workers in Alberta through its representation on the Minimum Wage Board. Union member Harriet J. Ingram served on the board from 1922 to 1924, and Lillian Morris from 1924 to 1934. However, Minimum Wage Board records from the period make it clear that the board always struggled to find a balance between the demands of employers and employees.

Local 120 members also raised issues of concern to working women through the Alberta Federation of Labour. For example, at the 1928 AFL Convention in Calgary, Annie Stephenson and Lillian Morris of Local 120 raised the case of the Maxine School of Beauty Culture in Calgary, which was employing girls for less than the minimum wage on the grounds that it was a school rather than a business. They wanted to prevent other employers from claiming that they were operating schools to avoid paying minimum wage. Great Western Garment had instructors on staff whose job it was to train new workers, but whether or not they were considering calling it a school cannot be determined.

The whole area of payment of apprentices was one which the Minimum Wage Board had difficulty enforcing. Board records indicate that because garment manufacturing required largely unskilled labour, manufacturing companies could have used more employees with less than a year's experience than the act allowed, but the employee representative on the board wanted to maintain jobs for more experienced workers.

Even though Great Western Garment promoted the fact that it was a union shop, the company occasionally outsourced production to another company or subcontractor, common practice in the garment manufacturing industry. In the 1920s Great Western Garment produced a limited range of goods, overalls, shirts, and pants, each requiring a different set-up on the cutting and sewing machines. It was sometimes difficult to estimate sales and to keep up with demand.

In 1925 the Edmonton Trades and Labour Council was advised that GWG garments were being produced in private homes and non-union firms. Local 120 delegates reported that garments were not being made in private homes. However, GWG had had some garments manufactured for them by Courtney Manufacturing, a small, non-unionized firm just down the street that made shirts, blouses, and overalls. The ETLC allowed Great Western Garment to do so, but garments produced there could only bear the GWG brand label, not the separate Union Made label.

The Alberta government revised the Factories Act in 1926, and in 1927 established an advisory committee to determine the minimum wage, maximum hours, and proportion of apprentices allowed. Great Western Garment was used as an example to the commission established to investigate the forty-eight-hour workweek (rather than the nine-hour day and fifty-four-hour week allowed under the Factories Act).

Consumer and Corporate Affairs records include letters from a number of non-unionized manufacturing companies in the province, such as LaFlèche Bros., the Calgary Knitting Company, and L.W. Caldwell Ltd. (hosiery), and their predominantly male workers, arguing against the eight-hour day and forty-four-hour week. The companies wrote that they needed to keep fewer skilled workers employed year-round, working overtime seasonally when required, rather than employ more workers during the busy season and lay them off periodically. The workers were prepared to work overtime

periodically in order to have year-round employment. LaFlèche Bros. associated the eight-hour day with companies paying on piecework. All noted competition from Eastern firms working longer hours for lower minimum wage.

The union's concerns during this period were for the welfare of working women, "maternal feminism" as it is known. For example, at the 1928 AFL Convention, Local 120 UGWA delegates sought to include provision for deserted wives and families under the Mothers' Allowance Act, and to introduce a four-month maternity leave for working women, two months before and two months after birth, with an allowance to be paid by the government. While the government eventually expanded the scope of the Mothers' Allowance, the AFL referred the resolution regarding maternity leave back to the Resolutions Committee and dropped the idea.

✕--------------✕

ABOVE: **Made in Alberta, 1928**
During the financially difficult 1920s, the city and the province promoted "Shop Locally" and "Made in Alberta" public awareness campaigns. This GWG booth was one of a number dedicated to local businesses at a Made in Alberta trade fair. PAA, A17805

EXPANSION OF THE GWG PLANT

Great Western Garment built a two-storey addition on the north side of the factory in 1925. The morning of May 10, 1926, GWG employees arrived at the plant to see firefighters struggling to put out a fire that would cost $250,000 and had started at 3:00 that morning. The *Edmonton Bulletin* reported that the fire began in the furnace room in the basement and spread through all three upper floors of the building before the fire department was able to extinguish it by 9:30 a.m. GWG laid off three hundred workers temporarily.

Fortunately, the fire did not damage the 1925 addition and the company was able to reopen quickly with just twenty-six machines. It took several months to acquire additional material and temporary premises, and to complete the restoration of the building, enabling the company to return to full production. GWG installed a sprinkler system to reduce potential future damage. The fire was just a temporary setback.

The following year GWG purchased the building and provided space for another one hundred machines by adding a fourth floor. GWG minimized the risk of fire in the plans for the addition by adding a fire escape to the fourth floor, modifying the stairway, and retrofitting the elevator. The fire department responded to a drill within fifty seconds of the alarm sounding. GWG also planned a two-storey addition to the back of the building, even before the company occupied the fourth floor.

Great Western Garment also acquired "Factory #2," a satellite location in the Tilley Press Ltd. building nearby at 9616-101A Avenue, that contained the mackinaw and leather departments.

Great Western Garment Addition, 1925
In 1925, the mackinaw and leather departments were separated from the overalls and pants departments because leather and sheepskin were handled differently than woven textiles and work was more seasonal than in other lines in the factory. Great Western Garment was able to shift production between overalls and pants with little difficulty, but as the company's product line expanded, it required more machines that were set up for different weights of fabric and operators with different expertise.
PAA, c. 1925, A9349

41

Great Western Garment Continued to Expand, 1927
After the 1927 expansion, the shipping and receiving department, and later the cafeteria, was in the basement. The business offices were on the first floor, the sewing machine operators on the second and third floors, and the cutters on the top floor. Each worker remained within his or her own sphere in the plant. They did not interact with workers in other departments. PAA, BI209.2

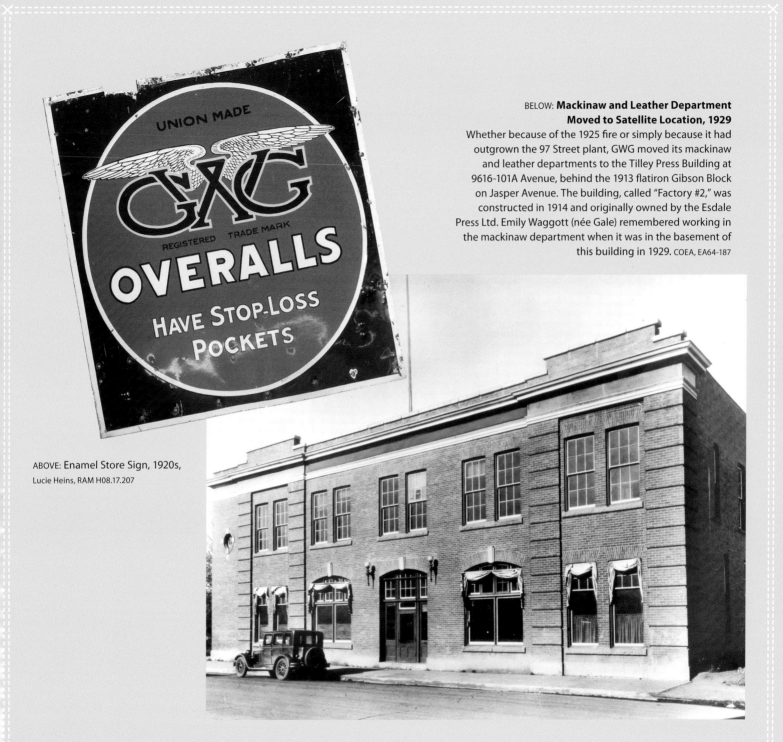

BELOW: **Mackinaw and Leather Department Moved to Satellite Location, 1929**

Whether because of the 1925 fire or simply because it had outgrown the 97 Street plant, GWG moved its mackinaw and leather departments to the Tilley Press Building at 9616-101A Avenue, behind the 1913 flatiron Gibson Block on Jasper Avenue. The building, called "Factory #2," was constructed in 1914 and originally owned by the Esdale Press Ltd. Emily Waggott (née Gale) remembered working in the mackinaw department when it was in the basement of this building in 1929. COEA, EA64-187

UNION MADE
GWG
REGISTERED   TRADE MARK
OVERALLS
HAVE STOP-LOSS
POCKETS

ABOVE: Enamel Store Sign, 1920s,
Lucie Heins, RAM H08.17.207

Labour Day Picnic at Alberta Beach, 1928
Labour Day celebrates the economic and social achievements of workers. Local 120 held its first annual Labour Day picnic at Alberta Beach in 1916. The men organized the sports and the women the refreshments. The Labour Day picnics provided a rare opportunity for workers and their families to enjoy a day together out of the city. Courtesy of Lillian Morris

The Label that means so much to you!

The famous G.W.G. winged label has become a symbol — a mark of
distinction identifying Canada's finest garments for all the family.
Behind this label is over 50 years of experience in creating strong,
sturdy garments embodying those qualities of longer wear and perfect
fit that Canadians in every walk of life have come to know and
appreciate. This trade-mark is your positive guide to the best value
for all the family!

* G.W.G. Brand Names are Registered Trade Marks

UNION   LABEL

* REG.

Canada's Finest Garments for Work and Casual Wear!

G.W.G. BRAND NAMES TO REMEMBER

* "COWBOY KING"
* "FRONTIER QUEEN"
* "FRISCO JEAN"
* "TEXAS RANGER"

Illustrated are:
"COWBOY KING"
Western Style Pants

"FRISCO JEAN"
Matched Outfit

THE GREAT WESTERN GARMENT CO. LTD., EDMONTON

46

Maclean's, June 9, 1956.
RAM

You're on the Right Track!... when you buy
G.W.G. *Quality* GARMENTS

Star Weekly,
March 15, 1958.
RAM

MORE *Value* FOR YOUR MONEY!

Shown here is the Western Style G.W.G. **SATEEN** Shirt Available in Scarlet, Black and Canary Yellow.

BUY YOUR CORRECT SIZE

G.W.G. Garments are styled in Graduated Sizes for all the family!

Correct fit means
**COMFORT
SMARTNESS
LONGER WEAR**

You can always get your correct size in G.W.G. garments.

They wear LONGER because they're made S-T-R-O-N-G-E-R!

The famous
***"RED STRAP"** Pant Overall
in quality ***"Snobak"** denim an exclusive G.W.G. fabric

G.W.G. EXPRESS STRIPE SLEEVELESS COVERALL

with zipper front fastening—the strong durable garment for every industrial job.

This label on the garment—your assurance of quality—always

UNION   LABEL

These are the Buy-Words with most Canadian families

G.W.G."*COWBOY KING*" Rider Pants   G.W.G. WOMEN'S"*FRONTIER QUEEN*" Slacks and Shirts
G.W.G."*TEXAS RANGER*" Shirts   G.W.G."*RED STRAP*" Bib Overalls
G.W.G."*FRISCO JEAN*" Matched Outfits   G.W.G."*DRILLER'S DRILL*" Matched Outfits

Most G.W.G. Garments are made for boys 'n girls too!

***REG.**   *G.W.G. BRAND NAMES ARE REGISTERED TRADE MARKS.

THE GREAT WESTERN GARMENT CO. LTD., EDMONTON

49

GWG Catalogue,
1938, p. 21. RAM

These are the famous G.W.G. "Blue Diamond" engineer shirts—every Blue Diamond shirt is "tops" in its class. They're Sanforized-shrunk. Sizes 14½ to 17½. Also extra sizes.

Zipper Styles

140-A Heavy weight grey chambray.
140-B Heavy weight dark blue chambray.
140-C Navy blue twill.
Price $1.75

Button Styles

133-D Heavy weight light blue chambray.
133-E Polka dot twill.
133-F Heavy weight grey chambray.
133-G Navy blue twill.
Price $1.75

WORK CLOTHES
Strong Sturdy — for the Toughest jobs

GWG UNION MADE

MEN'S "RED STRAP" PANTS

Sturdy denim in hard-wearing, neat-fitting pants that can take all the hard work you can give them.

Waist sizes 30 - 50, leg lengths 28 - 36.

63-01-7 Blue Denim, Button Fly
64-01-7 Blue Denim, Zipper Fly   **5.95**

THEY WEAR LONGER
BECAUSE THEY'RE
MADE STRONGER

MEN'S "RED STRAP" BIB OVERALLS

Tailored for superior comfort from tough, long wearing GWG denim in high or low back styles for free and easy movement. Sizes 34 - 50, short, medium, long.

21-01-7 Blue Denim, High Back _____7.50
25-01-7 Blue Denim, Zipper Front ____7.95
25-02-7 Express Stripe, Zipper Front __7.95
30-01-7 Blue Denim, Low Back _____7.50

MEN'S "RED STRAP" SMOCKS

Famous GWG "Red Strap" smocks to match the "Red Strap" pants. Four large pockets, stoutly double-stitched and reinforced at points of strain. Sizes 36 - 50.

29-01-7 Blue Denim, Short _____5.95
22-01-7 Blue Denim, Long _____7.50

MEN'S COVERALLS

A top quality coverall with special comfort features and long, hard-wearing quality. Made from strong express stripe denim and exclusive GWG twill, pre-shrunk for easy washing.

Sizes 34 - 50, short, medium, long.

27-02-7 Express Stripe, Button Front
27-40-7 Olive Herringbone, Button Front
28-40-7 Olive Herringbone, Zipper Front
28-42-7 Spruce Green, Zipper Front   **9.95**

CARPENTERS' OVERALLS

Made from GWG's exclusive unbleached, unshrunk twill with every comfort and utility feature. Double stitched and reinforced throughout. Sizes 34 - 50, short, medium, long.

26-70-7 _____7.95

GWG Catalogue, 1965, p. 10. RAM

51

1930-1939

CHAPTER TWO

- -

GREAT WESTERN GARMENT BEGAN 1930 on a note of optimism. C.A. Graham's Monthly Trade Letter dated January 2, 1930, while acknowledging the stock market crash, referred to the sound base of Western Canada's prosperity in the late 1920s. He stated that the situation did not compare to the depression of 1920-21: "none of the symptoms of ill-health, which were so plain ten years ago, now call for attention."

He continued to remain optimistic throughout 1931. Rather than retrench, he announced the establishment of a new department to produce fine broadcloth shirts, labelled the Graham Shirt. He also recruited Clarence D. Jacox from Seattle as general manager (a position Jacox held until 1941 when he became president). Jacox refined the assembly line system in the plant, increased efficiency by dividing the construction of garments into more operations, and introduced piecework incentives.

However, the impact of the Depression began to be felt as sales and profits declined in the early 1930s. The company survived through diversification, improved manufacturing methods, and cooperation with labour. As Graham had observed during the 1920 recession, unlike the fashion industry, workwear manufacturing is fairly depression-resistant. Work clothing wears out through use and needs to be replaced periodically. Traditionally, garment manufacturing requires a relatively small capital investment; most of the overhead cost is labour.

Still, Great Western Garment had to cut wages and lay off operators during slow periods. Given the difficulty of finding another job, the operators were grateful to have a job at all. Many women were the primary breadwinners in their families as their husbands were either unable to find work or were absent, incapable, or abusive. Elizabeth Shinbine worked at the plant throughout her marriage, taking as little as two weeks off to have a baby. Her co-workers teased her saying, "We don't have to worry about Beth, she's got the box [the box which held the bundles] right there, she'll have it and then she'll go back to work." Her husband, a printer by trade, was often unable to find work of any sort and would stay home to care for the children.

For other local manufacturers, the struggles were more extreme. At Reynolds Manufacturing, Harold Reynolds returned to work as a cook at the Metropolitan Store during the day and continued to manufacture garments in his basement at night. His son Lloyd joined the firm in the mid-1930s and remembered just how hand to mouth the business was: "Waitresses...bought their own uniforms in those days for $2.75 each at weekly instalments of $0.25. I picked up their quarters on Wednesdays so we could pay our girls on Thursdays."

General Whitewear was established in the basement of the Alberta Hotel in 1935 because "there were no jobs to be had," so the family created jobs for themselves. Roberta Watson (née Walsh) and her brother Arthur McIntyre joined their father, former salesman Robert W. McIntyre, in the business.

In 1932 Great Western Garment lobbied the government to introduce a six-month probationary period during which they could pay operators piecework rates even if they fell below the minimum wage. The government introduced a handicapping system to allow GWG to pay 10 percent to 25 percent less than minimum wage to individual workers or to entire production lines transferred from one type of work to another. A number of women working at the plant were suffering from accidents, illness, or chronic conditions that impacted their work and also required handicaps. Government records detailed their hardships.

Cowboy Kings

Introduced in 1929, the Cowboy King brand was relatively expensive compared to other workwear brands. For example, ranch hands earned $0.25 a day with room and board; a pair of Cowboy King pants cost $2.25, the equivalent of nine days' work. Although the clothing cost more to buy, Great Western Garment argued that it would last longer and therefore require replacement less often than other brands.

Throughout the 1930s, Great Western Garment registered a number of patents and trademarks, features such as Stop-Loss pockets (1930) and the Lochbar suspender slide (1936), and the brand names that would become its staples: Red Strap (1932), Iron Man (1932), Husky (1936), and Texas Ranger (1937).

In 1932 Great Western Garment acquired an interest in Canadian Cottons Ltd., holding a $115,000 mortgage on its new plant in Cornwall, Ontario. Jacox worked closely with the textile mill to develop better quality fabrics, stronger

AT THE CALGARY STAMPEDE...

COWBOYS ARE KINGS

The picture proves that, to a man, Westerners go for G.W.G. "Cowboy-King" Pants and Jackets.

Actual Scene Photographed at the 1945 Calgary Stampede, Champion Chuck Wagon Outfit

IT'S FREE!
A new, 1946 G.W.G. ALMANAC!
Send your name and address now, for this entertaining edition of G.W.G. ALMANAC — filled with more and more pages of dreams. 1946 horoscopes, gardening, farm and household hints, teacup reading, and a dozen fascinating new subjects. Send your name and address to The Great Western Garment Company, Edmonton, Alberta.

THE GREAT WESTERN GARMENT COMPANY, LTD., EDMONTON

Cowboy King, 1929
The Cowboy King brand was registered in 1929 but did not appear regularly in advertisements until the 1940s. Cowboy Kings were rider style pants and jackets and Western style shirts, but they did not initially have a separate brand label so may be difficult to identify. Men's Cowboy Kings were made of Buckskin denim, whereas women's and boys' were made of Snobak denim. Cowboy King eventually became one of the most popular GWG brands in the company's history.
Country Guide, June 1946. RAM

Christmas during the Depression

Before World War II, Christmas was primarily a religious event, not the commercialized celebration that it has become since. People gave and received very few presents, and those they did exchange tended to be practical gifts: slippers, the proverbial tie, and work clothing were good choices. This 1930 Hudson's Bay Company advertisement for GWG noted that the gift of GWG clothing was not only the gift of high-quality clothing, but also helped to provide work for Edmontonians. *Alberta Labor News*, December 15, 1930, p. 4. PAA

Stop-Loss Pockets, 1930
GWG introduced Stop-Loss pockets on the overall bib and pant leg to prevent the loss of pocket watches and tools, proclaiming, "Nothing can fall out of Stop-Loss pockets." The combination pockets were side-opening hip pockets and top-opening tool-and-rule-pockets. *The Nor'-West Farmer*, February 20, 1930, p. 47. Reynolds-Alberta Museum

Iron Man, 1932
Introduced in 1932, Iron Man pants and jackets were available either pre-shrunk or not and were made of a durable, good-looking, heavyweight fabric that wore like iron, and was manufactured specifically for GWG. Iron Man pants were relatively easy for the operators to work on because the fabric kept its shape. The Iron Man brand was popular until about 1960. *GWG Catalogue*, 1938, p. 7. RAM

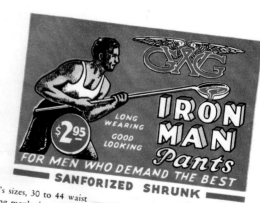

Red Strap, 1932

In 1932 GWG registered its signature: contrasting strap across the bib pocket of overalls and hammer strap across the pant leg. Red Straps soon became very popular. Even without a distinct brand label, Red Straps are easy to identify because of the straps, often printed onto bib pockets of early jackets. The hammer strap on pants and overalls did not just provide a handy place to keep a hammer. In the 1950s it was a challenge for teenage boys growing up in Edmonton's inner city to keep the red straps on their pants. Schoolyard bullies tried to rip them off and it became a mark of a boy's "ability to look after himself" if he managed to keep his red straps. GWG Catalogue, 1938, p. 1. RAM

RED STRAP
OVER-ALLS

G.W.G. for me! say thousands and thousands of Westerners who know inferior garments are expensive at any price. G.W.G. garments are never built down to a price—everything that is required to make long wearing, good looking and properly fitting garments is put into them, whether for men, women or children—whether for work, dress or sports and then the lowest price possible, consistent with high quality, is put on G.W.G. garments.

You can always trust a G.W.G. garment to give you the best of service — they never let you down — you know they wear well—your friends know they look well on you.

Snobak, 1935

Registered in 1935, Snobak was a good quality, pre-shrunk, 2.2 twill (meaning each weft thread passes over or under two warp threads), heavyweight denim that was blue on the right side and white on the reverse. Snobak blue denim was used for pants, overalls, and from 1939 particularly Red Straps, and later girls' and boys' Cowboy Kings. GWG Catalogue, 1938, p. 2. RAM

and more colourfast. Great Western Garment developed Buckskin, Iron Man (1932), and Snobak denim (1935) fabrics in collaboration with Canadian Cottons Ltd. Great Western Garment was the first Canadian firm to use fabrics made using the Sanforized compressive shrinkage process. The word Sanforized came from inventor Sanford L. Cluett, and the process was patented in the United States in 1930. Earlier striped overall denim had stripes made of rows of pinpoint dots printed on a cotton that, as Max Bedard recalled, "would shrink up to nothing" if you boiled it. Before World War II, workwear was always GWG's main focus. But the plant was flexible enough that GWG could produce whatever people would buy. In 1932 GWG began producing clothing for youth, and in 1934 expanded into women's wear in a modest way. In total, GWG produced more than seven hundred individual lines of garments. GWG also manufactured uniforms for

city workers and filled orders of overalls for the City of Edmonton's Special Relief Department, clothing that was given to approximately two thousand families and eighty single women during the Depression. One worker from 1928 to 1931, Emily Waggott, even remembered making cotton sanitary pads.

The Stevens Commission

In 1934 the federal government established a Royal Commission on Price Spreads and Mass Buying—also known as the Stevens Commission after its chair, Harold Stevens—in response to the impact of mass buyers, such as Eaton's, that used their buying power to undercut smaller, independent stores and reduce manufacturers' revenues. The commission heard from manufacturers across the country, including

Texas Ranger shirts are made of a good strong cotton material that will wear and wear—they can be worn for either work or dress and will give complete satisfaction.

Note the neat buttoned-down collar. Sizes 14½ to 17½. Specify the color you want by number.

135-A. 135-B., etc. Price, $1.75

20

Texas Ranger, 1937

Texas Ranger shirts were one of GWG's most popular brands for more than thirty years from 1937. Consumers grew to trust the Texas Ranger brand and GWG introduced Texas Ranger matched sets. In the 1968 catalogue, GWG claimed they were Canada's "most popular matched sets." GWG Catalogue, 1938, p. 20. RAM

Super Quality "Husky" (REG.) Shirts
SANFORIZED-SHRUNK

The "Zeromole" material used in these shirts has a fine satiny finish on the face, and a warmly napped back and is heavy enough for almost any purpose—yet they are an all year round favourite with men who want shirts that are heavier than average.

Numbers P24-A, B, etc. Sizes 14½ to 17½, price $2.25

24

Husky, 1936

GWG introduced Husky shirts in 1936. Made of Zeromole moleskin, with a satin finish on the front and a napped back for extra warmth, the fabric was also called Beavertail suede. Husky shirts were popular through the 1950s and later matched with Springbok pants. GWG Catalogue, 1939, p. 24. RAM

Edmonton's Great Western Garment and Northwestern Manufacturing, a much smaller company. Great Western Garment did not sell to Eaton's and other large stores at this time because very little markup was allowed on GWG clothing. Eaton's demanded manufactures cut their prices to allow a larger markup in exchange for placing large orders.

Great Western Garment's responses were similar to those of garment manufacturing companies in Eastern Canada. Great Western Garment supported efforts to improve the environment for manufacturers in Canada, and to regulate the industry through a code of ethics, standardization of hours, wages and working conditions, and cooperation with organized labour. These measures would place all garment manufacturing companies on a level playing field rather than allowing non-unionized companies to undercut unionized firms, selling at prices that were lower than unionized firms could afford to meet. In the 1930s manufacturers benefited from protective tariffs that ensured 95 percent of all men's clothing purchased in Canada was Canadian made.

Cooperation between management and labour continued to be important to GWG's success. One example was a trip that union activist Lillian Morris made to southern Alberta with a management team from GWG. She remembered wearing men's overalls to encourage solidarity with labourers in other unionized industries. Management and union together promoted the union label. UGWA even lobbied clergy to promote the union label in order to abolish sweatshops in the garment trade by buying union made clothing, including vestments and choir garments.

By 1935 Great Western Garment was optimistic that the worst of the Depression was over and introduced a prosperity program, bringing the number of workers back to 300 from 250. After several years of layoffs and part-time work, GWG celebrated its twenty-fifth anniversary in 1936 by committing to full-time employment for its staff.

When the Depression ended, Great Western Garment was in relatively good shape. Recognizing the sacrifices workers had made to keep the company solvent during hard times, in 1940 it was one of the first companies in the city to increase wages, 15 percent in the first two years. In an article about the huge wartime orders received by GWG in the *Edmonton Journal* April 18, 1942, the newspaper noted that GWG was the largest garment manufacturing company in the British Empire before the war. The company's multi-pronged strategy of diversification, improved production methods, and cooperation with labour had paid off.

The Texas Ranger Line

Yes... they WASH!

The fine-looking fabric in your Texas Ranger shirt is also TOUGH! It washes easily, because it is Sanforized-Shrunk. G.W.G. Texas Ranger Shirts are carefully designed and finished, to give you maximum comfort. They are equally practical for work or dress occasions.

(at dealers throughout Western Canada . . though still in limited quantities)

Just off the Press!

1947 Almanac
Presented by the Makers of
G.W.G. WORK CLOTHES

WRITE FOR IT—IT'S FREE

GWG

THE GREAT WESTERN GARMENT COMPANY, LTD., EDMONTON

Texas Ranger, 1937
GWG used the archival photograph of shirts hanging from a clothesline on the roof of the factory (as seen on opposite page) as the basis for this Texas Ranger ad featured in the *Country Guide*, March 1947. In the era before colour photography, GWG frequently provided artists with photographs of employees modelling GWG clothing or garments displayed in different ways, to be illustrated in full colour. *Country Guide*, March, 1947. PAA Bl1098

GWG BRANDS

Before World War II, GWG registered a limited number of brands with the Canadian Intellectual Property Office, Cowboy King (1929) and Red Strap (1933) being the most popular. Other early brands include Iron Man (1932), Golden West Jean (1934), Snobak (1935), Husky (1936), Westwool (1937), Texas Ranger (1937), Blue Diamond (1938), Pinto and El Charro (1939), and Sport Togs (1939/reintroduced 1950).

Cowboy King (1929)

Lucie Heins, RAM, H08.17.41

Lucie Heins, RAM, H08.17.33

Country Guide, June 1950. RAM

DOWN ON THE FARM
OR ON THE RANCH
IT'S

GWG

Red Strap OVERALLS
for longer wear!

RED STRAP

GWG
"RED STRAP" COVERALLS
Strong, sturdy denims and
hard-wearing twills
pre-shrunk for easy washing.
The ideal outdoor garment
for Fall and Winter.

GWG "RED STRAP"
BIB OVERALLS
Tailored for superior comfort
from tough, long-wearing
GWG denim in high or
low back styles.

*"They Wear Longer Because
They're Made Stronger"*

Featured at leading stores
Coast to Coast

THE GREAT WESTERN GARMENT
CO. LTD., EDMONTON

FAMILY HERALD, No. 17, Aug. 18, 1966 — 19

**RED STRAP
OVERALLS**

**LOOK · BETTER
LAST · LONGER**

The famous G.W.G. label on the Red Strap
Overall is your assurance of the finest investment in an overall you'll ever make. They're
STRONG because they're tailored from
"SNOBAK" denim . . . a tough, hard-wearing
fabric made from tightly twisted strands of cotton,
an exclusive G.W.G. fabric. What's more there's
special attention to seams, finished for long wear
and smooth surfaces to eliminate friction. You'll
appreciate the roomy pockets . . . . stapled
buttons . . . roominess where needed for easy
action on the job . . . and above all, neat
appearance always.

*The G.W.G. LABEL means months
of extra wear . . . the Red Strap
overall not only WEARS well—but
WASHES well too!*

Ask for G.W.G. Work Clothes at Your Dealers.

THEY WEAR LONGER BECAUSE THEY'RE MADE STRONGER

GWG

THE GREAT WESTERN GARMENT
COMPANY, LTD.,
EDMONTON

National Home Monthly, 1945. RAM

Red Strap (registered 1933, in use earlier)

Family Herald,
August 18, 1966.
Private Collection

Lucie Heins, RAM, H08.17.44

Farm Workshop Guide,
1947. RAM

GWG
Red Strap
STAPLED BUTTONS
OVERALLS
FAMOUS RED STRAP

SNOBACK DENIM

REINFORCED SEAMS

Your first impression of G.W.G. RED STRAP OVERALLS will be, "Good-looking" . . . but that's only part of the story.

G.W.G. RED STRAP OVERALLS are tailored from Snoback Denim—a fabric exclusive with G.W.G.—that is made from tightly twisted strands of cotton, woven to give extra-long wear.

G.W.G. RED STRAP OVERALLS have smooth seams, and big pockets, and they're cut to give maximum ease for your work.

G.W.G. RED STRAP OVERALLS are not plentiful yet, but when you CAN get them, the quality is always tops!

Iron Man (1932)

Star Weekly, October 13, 1951. RAM

Country Guide, August 1947. RAM

IRON MAN
Pants

"Iron Man" (Reg.) are made in men's and boys' sizes. The material is of special construction and found only in G.W.G. Iron Man pants.

It is made in high waist (as illustrated by model A) for young men, and standard waist (as illustrated by model B) for boys and men.

Iron Man pants are made of Sanforized-shrunk and unshrunk material. Identify the kind you prefer by the labels on the opposite page.

Order Men's standard waist unshrunk under Nos. A. 61, B. 61, C. 61, D. 61, E. 61, F. 61.

Order men's standard waist Sanforized shrunk under Nos. A. 61S, B. 61S, C. 61S, D. 61S, E. 61S, and F. 61S.

Order young men's high band style unshrunk under Nos. A. 567, B. 567, etc.

Order young men's high band style Sanforized-shrunk under Nos. A 567S, B. 567S, etc.

Order boys' unshrunk under Nos. A. 3, B. 3, etc.

Order boys' Sanforized-shrunk under Nos. A 3S, B. 3S, etc.

See opposite page for prices.

6

GWG Catalogue, 1938, p. 6. RAM

Country Guide, March 1946. RAM

G.W.G. "IRON MAN" PANTS

LOOK AT THE STYLE
FEEL THE FABRIC
CHOOSE YOUR COLOR
REALIZE THE COMFORT

G.W.G. IRON MAN PANTS wear longer, because they're made stronger!
They're still a little scarce, but they're worth waiting for

G.W.G. 1946 ALMANAC...
JUST OFF THE PRESS
A new, bigger edition of the G.W.G. Almanac... with your 1946 horoscope—gardening—palmistry—songs—better household and farm hints—and dozens of fascinating pages. IT'S FREE! Send your name and address to The Great Western Garment Company, Edmonton, Alberta.

Shown with G.W.G. IRON MAN Pants ... the G.W.G. TEXAS RANGER SHIRT

DEPAR

THE GREAT WESTERN GARMENT COMPANY, LTD., EDMONTON

Golden West Jean (1934)

GWG Catalogue, 1950, p. 20. RAM

GWG Catalogue,
1950, p. 46. RAM

Snobak (1935)

Lucie Heins, RAM, H08.17.29

Husky (1936)

Westwool (1937)

"WESTWOOL"

Haven't you always wanted to own a pair of pure fleece wool pants made of all Western Canadian wool?

Aren't you tired of spending your money for wool pants that don't wear because they are made of wool that was reclaimed from worn out garments, wool rags and clippings or partially from such wools?

A label may state that a garment is all wool—but does it say what kind of wool? Only pure fleece wool (wool that has never been used before) can give you the maximum value that you have the right to expect.

You can be sure of getting pants made of pure fleece 100% Western Canadian wool if you will ask us for G.W.G. "Westwool" pants.

You can identify "Westwool" pants by this label—look for it on the right hip pocket inside each pair and on the waist-band on the outside of each pair.

Western Canada wool has characteristics all its own and, we believe, is especially adapted to the climate in which it was produced.

On pages 15 and 16 we show in color a range of G.W.G. Westwool pants made of all pure fleece Western Canadian wool—wool that you or your fellow Westerner produced.

14

GWG Catalogue, 1939, p. 14. RAM

Country Guide, November 1944. RAM

G.W.G.
WESTWOOL
JACKETS

HEAVY DUTY MACKINAW JACKETS IN BRIGHT COLORS

TYPE I
Vancouver Stag-- with extra warmth in double yoke and double sleeves.

TYPE II
Cruiser coat with double yoke, and game pocket across back.

TYPE III
Button-fitted jacket, double yoke for extra warmth. Tightens at side band.

TYPE IV
Zippered jacket that is tailored to neat lines and comfortable fit. Zipper breast pocket.

Exclusive G.W.G. pure, warm WESTWOOL is the fabric.

THE GREAT WESTERN GARMENT COMPANY, LTD., EDMONTON

Country Guide, November 1946. RAM

PURE FLEECE
Western Canadian
WOOL TROUSERS

Made from Wool produced in
• MANITOBA
• SASKATCHEWAN
• ALBERTA
• BRITISH COLUMBIA

SERVICE WEIGHT "WESTWOOL" (REG.) TROUSERS

G.W.G. "WESTWOOL" (Reg.) trousers were introduced to Western Canadians only six months ago, yet today thousands of Western men are wearing them, and with more satisfaction than they have found before in woolen trousers.

Order your favorite pattern by number and letter as follows: P16-WW-A; P16-WW-B; P16-WW-C; P16-WW-D; P16-WW-E; P16-WW-F; and P16-WW-G. Sizes 32 to 44 waist; lengths 29 to 35.   Price $6.95

16

GWG Catalogue, 1939, p. 16. RAM

Texas Ranger (1937)

Country Guide,
March 1948. RAM

Country Guide,
April 1945. RAM

Country Guide,
August 1948. RAM

"TEXAS RANGERS"

THE G.W.G. "TEXAS RANGER" SHIRT is tough enough to see action on the farm . . . cool and light for hot weather. Attractive colors . . . smart details, such as pockets, buttonholes and shoulder lines. . . . and the cotton twill material that wears longer—this is the G.W.G. TEXAS RANGER SHIRT!

Illustrated are G.W.G. pants of famous "Snobak" denim—G.W.G. Iron Man Pants—and G.W.G. khaki pants . . . all made for both men and boys.

When you see this—

TEXAS RANGER

you know it's the Best!

TEXAS RANGER Shirts

They WON'T SHRINK!
Wash them all you like you won't wash out the permanent fit, size or styling. They'll ALWAYS look neat and fit smoothly because they're SANFORIZED SHRUNK.

Texas Ranger Shirts give you double purpose service. They're neat and good looking for dress wear—yet tough and strong for rugged every day work. Here's your biggest dollars worth in a shirt that will stand by you with long, satisfactory service.

Six sparkling new colours in attractive herringbone design are now available in the famous TEXAS RANGER line. See them at the G.W.G. dealer near you.

THE GREAT WESTERN GARMENT COMPANY, LTD., EDMONTON

Farm Workshop Guide, 1946. RAM

Country Guide,
September 1950. RAM

73

Blue Diamond
(registered 1938, name in use from 1921)

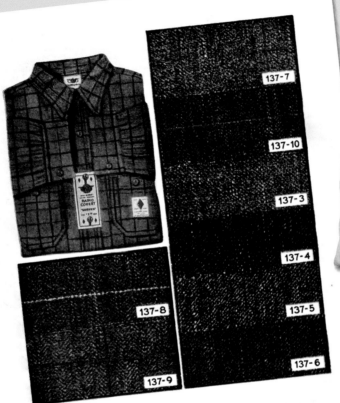

Blue Diamond "Radio Covert" Shirts

G.W.G. "Blue Diamond" Radio Covert Shirts are "shrunk". Good materials and good workmanship combine to make this line an outstanding value. Sizes 14½ to 17½, each $1.75

Pinto (1939)
El Charro (1939)

Sport Togs (1939/1950)

These styles are as Western as the Prairies and Mountains

(Left)

"Pinto" Shirts are made of a very high quality sateen. The wide collar, laced front, inserted pocket and long gauntlet cuff makes this a very popular number. Sizes 14½ to 17½.
Number P25-A, B, and C.
Price $2.25
Boys' sizes, ages 6 to 10.
Price $1.65
Ages 11 to 16, price $1.85

(Right)

"El Charro" is an old favourite with young men of the West. They are made of the same high quality sateen used in "Pinto" shirts. Note the novelty pockets and three-button cuff. Sizes 14½ to 17½.
Number P25-D, E, and F.
Price $2.45
Boys' sizes, ages 6 to 10.
Price $1.75
Ages 11 to 16, price $1.95

25

GWG Catalogue, 1939, p. 25. RAM

Lucie Heins, RAM, H08.17.140

Lucie Heins, RAM, H08.17.140

After the war, the company expanded its product lines, introducing Driller's Drill (1948), Frisco Jeans (1949), Palomino (1950), Graham (1950), High Rigger (1951), Beavertail (1953), Frontier Queen (1956), Springbok (1959), Strapback (1959), GWG Kings (1963), Ranch Boss (1959), Nev'R Press (1968), Peace Jeans (c. 1970), George W. Groovey (1970) and Grace W. Groovey (1970) brands. Some of these were trademarked, some not.

Driller's Drill (1948)

Maclean's, October 15, 1955

Country Guide, August 1950. RAM

Frisco Jeans (1949)

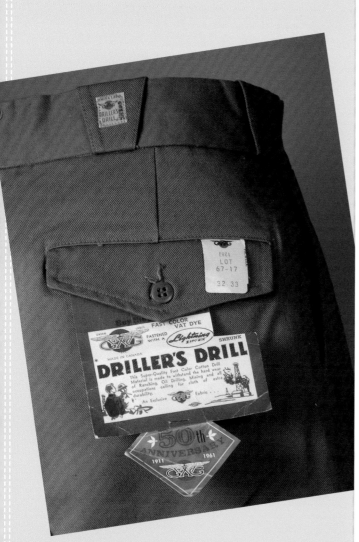

Lucie Heins, H08.17.57

GWG Catalogue, 1950, p. 27. RAM

Palomino (1950)

104-5

A western shirt tailored in quality English 10 oz. gabardine shirting, exclusive to G.W.G. in Canada. Neat form fitting body eliminating bunching or creeping, buttons are pearl in matching colors —neat dressy collar—pleated back for freedom and comfort in the body.

Sizes 14½ to 17½.

$19.50

64

104-2

104-3

104-5   104-1   104-4   104-6

Lucie Heins, RAM, H08.17.147

Lucie Heins, RAM, H08.17.147

GWG Catalogue, 1950, p. 24. RAM

Frontier Queen
(1956)

Country Guide,
April 1956. RAM

Strap Back (1959)

Lucie Heins, RAM, H08.17.74

Star Weekly, April 19, 1958. RAM

GWG Kings (1963)

GWG Catalogue, 1965, p. 2. RAM

GWG Catalogue, 1968, p. 5. RAM

GWG Catalogue, 1981, p. 13. RAM

Nev'R Press (1968)

Lucie Heins,
RAM, H08.17.69

Lucie Heins, RAM, H08.17.69

George W. Groovey (1970)

Lucie Heins, RAM, H08.17.47

Grace W. Groovey
(1970)

GWG Catalogue,
1970, p. 7. RAM

Fashion Flares that catch the eye and fit the figure.

GRACE W. GROOVEY FLARES.

Co-ordinated slacks, skirts and boleros to make your own image or match the male of your choice! Bold Stripes — Bleach-outs — Tie-Dyes — Pinto Denims. For what's new and different, see your GWG dealer—he has the latest in style and fabric. Here's just a few:

22. RANCH TWILL — Flared jeans in plain shade cotton twill, fully machine-washable. White, Turqua, Blue, Sand, Brown, Avocado. Sizes 8 to 18, 38 and 40. Short, Medium or Long ----------------------- 7.95

NEV'R-PRESS CANVAS — with one-year guarantee. Fortrel/Cotton in Blue, Brown, Avocado or Gold. Sizes 8 to 18. Short, Medium or Long ------------ 9.95

23. WIDE TRACKS — basketweave Cotton and Nylon fabric that styles nicely in flared jeans. White ground with wide-coloured stripes in Blue, Brown, Green, Gold or Maroon.
SIZES 8 to 18, Short, Medium or Long ----- 10.95

PINTO DENIM—GWG's exclusive bleached-out, sueded, Blue Cotton Denim in co-ordinated bolero, skirt or jeans.

24. Bolero top, sizes 10 to 16 ------------ 8.00

25. Wrap-around mini skirt,
Misses' sizes 8 to 16 ------------------ 9.00

26. Jeans—misses' sizes 8 to 18,
Short, Medium or Long -------------------- 10.95
Girls' sizes—7 to 14 -------------------- 8.95

GRACE W. GROOVEY FLARES. Evasés dernier cri qui attirent les regards et flattent le corps. Pantalons co-ordonnés, jupes et boléro pour vous plaire ou pour s'harmoniser à l'homme de votre choix! Bold Stripes, Bleach-outs, Tie-Dyes, Denims Pinto. Pour le nouveau et le différent—voyez votre concessionnaire GWG—il a toutes les nouveautés. En voici quelques exemples:

22. RANCH TWILL—Jeans évasés en cotons croisés unis entièrement lavables à la machine. Blanc, turquoise, bleu, sable, brun, avocat.
TAILLES 8 à 18, 38 et 40. Courtes, Moyennes ou Longues --------------------------------------- 7.95

NEV'R-PRESS CANVAS—Un an de garantie—en Fortrel /coton bleu, brun, avocat ou or.
TAILLES 8 à 18. Courtes, Moyennes ou Longues 9.95

23. WIDE TRACKS — Tissu "basketweave" coton et nylon, donnant une coupe parfaite aux jeans évasés. Fond blanc à larges lignes bleu, brun, vert, or ou marron.
TAILLES 8 à 18. Courtes, Moyennes, Longues.. 10.95

PINTO DENIM—Décoloration exclusive GWG—suédine de coton bleu existant en coordonnés boléro, jupe ou jeans.

24. Dessus boléro.
TAILLES 10 à 16 ---------------------------- 8.00

25. Mini-jupe enveloppante.
TAILLES 8 à 16 pour jeunes filles ----------- 9.00

26. Jeans—tailles 8 à 18 pour jeunes filles. Courtes, Moyennes, Longues ---------------------------- 10.95
TAILLES 7 à 14 pour fillettes ------------- 8.95

In 1972 GWG introduced what would become the most popular brand in its history, Scrubbies. Other late brands include: Flare Kings (1972), Jeanslax (1978), Cachet Cadet (1979), Kidfitters (1979), Femme Fit (1980), Great Western Jeans (1980), Poupounette (1980), Pionnier (1980), Bum Bums and Bum Jeans (1978), Odyssey (1982), Rugby (1982), British Khaki (1982), Canadian Wilderness Gear (1990), and Tradition of Excellence (1991). Many of these were quickly abandoned.

Scrubbies (1972)

Lucie Heins,
RAM, H08.17.28

Pre-washed | Déjà lavés
Ready to wear | Prêts-a-porter
FLARES
GWG
SCRUBBIES

Lucie Heins,
RAM, H08.17.28

Lucie Heins, RAM, H08.17.28

Flare Kings (1972)

Lucie Heins, RAM, H08.17.28

Femme Fit (1980)

Lucie Heins, RAM, H08.17.45

1939-1946

SOON AFTER WORLD WAR II broke out in September 1939, the Great Western Garment Company dedicated two-thirds of its production to government contracts. Great Western Garment played an important role during the war. The company had built its business and reputation on high-quality workwear and fair labour practices, a combination that was essential to its success in securing government contracts.

Great Western Garment produced up to twenty-five thousand pieces of military clothing a week, including army combinations, khaki shorts and shirts, khaki battle dress uniforms, pants for the army, the RCAF, and the navy, ground crew combinations, uniforms for explosives workers, prisoner-of-war uniforms, and military uniforms for other countries.

The plant was in full production. Two—and in the summer of 1940, even three—shifts of operators worked around the clock when necessary. Workers frequently worked overtime to fill contracts and GWG reduced the number of holidays.

Founder Charles A. Graham died at the age of fifty-eight in December 1940 and Clarence D. Jacox became president. Ownership of the company was consolidated in the Graham (and his in-laws, the Shaws) and Jacox families.

In 1941, GWG's thirtieth anniversary, the accumulated value of GWG's government contracts reached $1 million. The increase in production prompted GWG to expand the plant again. In 1942 GWG built a $125,000 two-storey addition to the east of the plant.

The workforce expanded from four hundred to five hundred people. The union was often initiating twenty or thirty new members a month. Many of these new workers were recent immigrants. Former operators remember that at this time an increasing number of women working in the plant did not speak English. As former operator and union activist Anne Ozipko said, "Ukrainian women, Italian women, very few of them spoke English. Everybody talked their own language."

Canadian-born women who worked at the plant often started just out of high school, or took the job when they moved to the city from farms in the surrounding area. Some took the job to support the war effort, or to support their fiancés and husbands who were serving overseas; others were helping to support their parents and siblings.

Former operator Assunta Dotto (née Peron) remembered that it was a "source of good employment for immigrants during the wartime and even after the war because…we were not able to get employment any other way." She noticed that the women working at the plant who were born in Canada complained, but she "saw the GWG as a lifesaver because it got [her] a start."

Canadian-born workers noted that the immigrant women were harder working than they were. Operator Helen Allen joked, "They wouldn't even take time to go to the washroom. They were just givin' her, you know."

Jobs within the garment manufacturing industry were

Labour Day Picnic, September 2, 1942
During World War II, the workers went to Gull Lake, southwest of Edmonton, for a Labour Day picnic. Former employees Nellie Engley and Emma Gilbertson remembered having fun with their friends from the plant. They took the CPR train from the station at 109 Street and Jasper Avenue, got off by the lake, ate, went for a walk, took off their shoes, and spent a relaxing afternoon on the beach. The train stopped on its way into Edmonton to pick them up again.
FRONT TO BACK: Hertha Fleming's daughter, Melinda Haas, Esther Mayan, Nellie Engley, and Ruth Arndt. Photograph by Hertha Fleming. Courtesy of Nellie Engley

GWG Factory Continues to Expand
In 1942 GWG added a $125,000 two-storey addition to the east, modified the exterior of the building, and moved Jacox's office and the administration and sales departments from the factory to the addition. This allowed the company to accommodate one hundred more operators in the plant. Photograph by Alfred Blyth, December 1944. PAA, BL814.7

Interior of Addition
The addition also included a sample room. GWG periodically allowed employees to shop at a discount for clothing for their own personal use. Photograph by Alfred Blyth, December 1944. PAA, BL814.2

Staff of The Great Western Garment

GWG's Thirtieth Anniversary
One Saturday afternoon in October 1941, hundreds of GWG staff lined up outside the plant for a panoramic photograph to commemorate the company's thirtieth anniversary. The front row includes the floor lady Annie Stephenson (left), president Clarence D. Jacox (centre), at the end of the group of men,

ALLS · SHIRTS

Housez STUDIOS EDMONTON

ny Ltd., Edmonton, Alberta. 1941

and other members of the management and office staff. The
Edmonton Journal published this photograph April 18, 1942.

Photograph by Alfred Blyth. Courtesy of Helen Allen

**Women Worked
as Cutters during the War**
Unknown, Ellen Klapstein
(née Cox), and Beulah Williams
(née Nelson) (LEFT TO RIGHT) worked as
cutters during World War II. In 1942 Nelson
was working as a presser when GWG offered
her the opportunity to become a cutter, with
more respect, better pay, hourly wages, and
more variety. The plant's tailor made them
each a pair of pants to wear on the job, so
they could dress like men while doing men's
work. When the men returned after the war,
GWG expected the women to return to their
former positions. Nelson married and
chose to leave the plant.
Courtesy of Beulah Williams

Cutters sometimes went out on the
rooftop to relax during their breaks.
Senior male cutters, who were too old to
enlist, remained working at the plant.
They tackled the more challenging
fabrics and designs. LEFT TO RIGHT: Iola
Jones, Lloyd Pontney, Bob Ritchie,
Charley Quinn, and Alf Cameron.
Courtesy of Beulah Williams

normally divided along gender lines. In general, women worked as bundle girls, machine operators, examiners, pressers, instructors, and office workers, and men worked as designers, tailors, cutters, packers, mechanics, and salesmen. However, during the war, gender lines blurred as women replaced some of the young men from the plant who enlisted in the armed forces.

Cutters were relatively well paid compared to other positions. The fabric arrived in huge bales and was taken up to the top floor of the plant in the elevator. The cutter and a helper laid out sixty layers of fabric: twenty layers, then a piece of paper, twenty more layers and another piece of paper, then the final twenty layers with the pattern on top. All of the pieces for each size of garment were cut from the same dye lot to make sure that they were exactly the same colour. They had to make sure that the piles stayed straight so that when they were cut every piece was exactly the same. They were careful not to make any mistakes because they were cutting through sixty layers of fabric at a time and mistakes were costly.

"Fighting Hitler with Needles"

In a radio broadcast, August 1942, Prime Minister William Lyon Mackenzie King introduced the national selective service program to monitor labour in the war effort. King encouraged factory workers who were supporting the military effort through their wartime production: "every man and woman capable of performing some form of war service should undertake the service for which he or she may be best qualified and when the demands of war require.... Every person must regard his services as essential to the combined effort.

CLARENCE D. JACOX, 1945

Clarence Jacox was born in Pennsylvania. He worked in Pittsburgh's steel mills from the age of fourteen, and later in retail clothing and manufacturing. In 1914 he moved to Seattle to work as a clothing salesman.

He was recruited by GWG as general manager in 1931 and became president and managing director after Charles A. Graham died in 1940.

C.D. Jacox was well respected within GWG by both unionized workers and his management team. Workers considered him to be fair and to have the best interests of his staff at heart. Local 120 and C.D. Jacox had an unusually good relationship. In 1950 employees presented him with an engraved clock to express their appreciation for his role in negotiating satisfactory agreements. He improved working conditions and wages, health and sanitation, pension plans, and welfare funds.

In addition to his work with GWG, he served on the Wartime Prices and Trade Board during World War II, the Canadian Garment Manufacturers' Association, the Calgary Exhibition and Stampede, and the Edmonton Chamber of Commerce.

He died in March 1958 and was succeeded by J. Gerald Godsoe.

Photograph by Alfred Blyth. PAA, BL872

Cutting, 1942
In the early years, the cutters did not wear dust masks or protective gloves, and the knives were very sharp and dangerous and did not have guards. Their hands would turn blue from the dye in the denim. Once the pieces were cut, they were tied into bundles and a bundle boy or girl delivered them to the machine operators. This photograph shows long-term employees Percy Williamson (FRONT) and Charley Quinn (REAR) laying out patterns to be cut. Photograph by Harry Rowed. LAC/National Film Board fonds/e002505379

Wartime Propaganda and the GWG Factory, 1942
Between 1939 and 1945, the federal government took more than twenty-five thousand images of various home-front activities in Canada to inform the public and encourage support of the war effort. Called the War Records-Manufacturing (WRM) series, the government distributed prints to weekly newspapers and other publications. In 1943 the photography section of the Wartime Information Board became a part of the National Film Board. This is one of a series of photographs showing GWG workers making servicemen's uniforms, from laying out cloth, to placing patterns, cutting, and separating pieces into bundles, sewing, checking work in progress, inspecting, folding and bundling, and preparing garments for shipment. Photographer Harry Rowed. LAC/National Film Board fonds/e002505382

WRM-1768

Occupational Health

The nurse provided a liaison between management and the union regarding workers' health and safety. The union provided food hampers and small amounts of money out of union dues to needy workers who were sick, to tide them over until they were able to return to work. The nurse provided health care advice and items like cold tablets at a good price. This photograph was one of a series published in the 1945 *GWG Almanac* promoting the modern factory. PAA, November 18, 1943. BL664.5

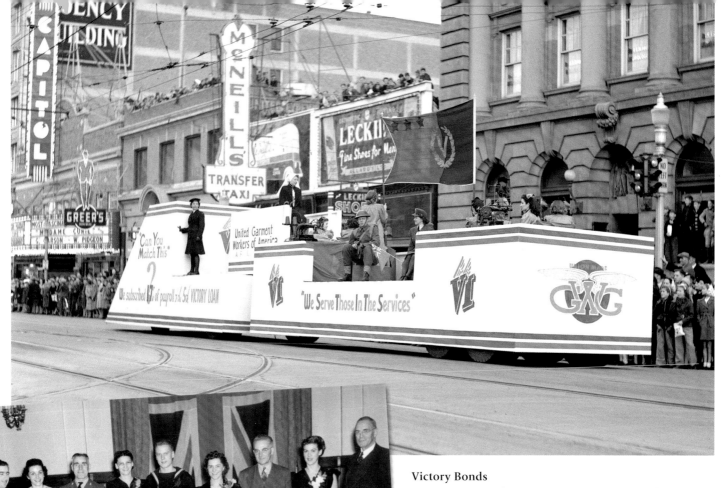

Victory Bonds

ABOVE: GWG employees supported Victory Bond campaigns. The *Edmonton Journal* noted June 5, 1941, that Great Western Garment workers oversubscribed their quota of Victory Bonds by 25 percent. In 1943 GWG workers were featured on a float in a workers' parade with the slogan "We Serve Those in the Service" to encourage Edmontonians to purchase Victory Bonds. PAA, Bl732.1

LEFT: At GWG's annual union-management banquet held at the MacDonald Hotel, December 10, 1943, the company thanked employees for their support of the Victory Bonds sales. Nellie Engley, financial secretary and Grace Trivett, vice-president of Local 120 are standing on either side of Clarence Jacox, who is third from the right. Victory Bonds banquet, 1943. Courtesy of Nelly Engley

Moreover, all should realize that the lives of our fighting men at sea, on land and in the air depend on men for the reinforcement of their ranks and on unremitting toil on the farm, in the mine, in the forest, in the mill and the factory, and on the merchant ships."

The government's manpower policy was discussed at union meetings, and former operators remembered being told they should not quit their jobs without a valid reason unless they enlisted because their work was considered an essential wartime service. Norah Hook remembered that when she told GWG she was quitting and going to work at Aircraft Repair Ltd., she was initially told she could not because her work at GWG was an essential service. Her mother intervened, and because she was only seventeen and working in another wartime industry, she was allowed to change jobs.

Marriage and childbirth often interrupted women's working lives. If they did not have family members able to help, employees had difficulty finding adequate childcare. In 1943 GWG supported a request from its workers that the city provide childcare and lobbied city council unsuccessfully on their behalf.

The contribution of GWG workers to the war effort was a source of pride for the community at the time. An article in the *Edmonton Bulletin*, February 4, 1942, noted, "Thousands of Canadian women are fighting Hitler with needles!" Canadians were encouraged to buy Victory Bonds, the precursor to Canada Savings Bonds, to help the Canadian government fund the war effort. The union and workers at the plant supported the war effort by buying Victory Bonds and sending money to plant workers serving overseas at Christmas, and cigarettes to "the boys" at Easter. Passwords at union meetings were occasionally war-related, such as "Onward to Victory." One woman mentioned putting her name and address in a uniform pocket, thinking the soldier who was issued it might like someone to communicate with,

but the note was caught before it left the plant and she was told not to do it again.

Working Conditions

Tuberculosis, a bacterial infection in the lungs, was a significant problem at the time, and the government brought Aboriginal people from the North and from surrounding reserves to Edmonton for treatment. Early diagnosis through X-rays was critical in reducing the spread of the disease. The 1936 Tuberculosis Act made diagnosis and treatment free for all Albertans. In 1942 the government X-rayed workers at the plant, screening for tuberculosis, as GWG had a large workforce working in close proximity to one another. Beulah Nelson remembered that they found some TB-infected people working in the plant and took them away. She remembered one girl in particular, "then she had TB and I don't think she ever came back." Antibiotics became available as a cure for TB in the 1940s, but the disease continued to be prevalent until the late 1950s. In 1944 GWG hired a full-time, on-site nurse and made a doctor available to workers on a part-time basis.

Beginning in the 1940s, GWG used efficiency experts, including the American George S. May International Co., to "speed up" the manufacturing process. They presented time-motion studies to the operators, divided sewing operations into many different steps, and taught operators how to complete each one. Engineers visited the plant to identify means to improve efficiency, introducing new construction techniques and procedures. Norah Hook commented about the assembly line, "I never saw my back end of the jeans after they left. They left, carted away."

Former operator Effie Hobden remembered the 1943 visit of an efficiency expert who came to "pass judgement" on the operation. Although GWG trained some operators on two machines so they could fill in for others when necessary, the union continued to prevent them from learning too many operations because, under the piecework system, they could earn more by perfecting one operation. GWG introduced more automated machinery and efficient production methods, and output grew from 7,000 to 12,500 uniforms per week—almost as many garments as it produced each year fifteen years earlier.

In 1942 Great Western Garment cut workers' rates as part of the government's effort to control wartime inflation, appealing to the workers' sense of patriotism. At the same time, the company continued to expand and prosper. Union meeting minutes record that the union wanted recognition of its partnership in the war effort.

In 1943 Local 120 UGWA President Emily Ross and ETLC representative Carl Berg went to the National War Labor Board to appeal the decision of the Alberta War Labor Board, which had sided with the company, and restore operators' rates. Local 120 won the dispute and wages were increased by 17.8 percent.

In 1944 the company tried to introduce a unit system of determining pay rates for each line based upon percentages, rather than following the ticket system previously in place. Operators who worked faster than others were unhappy with the new approach as they earned the average rate. Under the ticket system, workers collected tickets for each bundle of work completed. Their pay was based upon the number of tickets submitted. Those who completed the most work earned the most pay. GWG paid some jobs, such as instructors, hourly wages. Whether they were paid piecework or through the unit system, some women preferred to be paid for work completed rather than hourly wages because if they worked hard they could earn more money.

Nellie Engley remembered that experienced operators would rush to finish a bundle and then try to take another bundle that was of small-sized clothing. "Well, the older girls were smarter and they would pick out all the small sizes and leave the big ones for the new girls and of course…

Blacksmith's Cowboy King Jacket, c. 1936-1940s
Worn work clothing in museum collections is rare. This jacket is particularly rare. It came from a blacksmith's shop in an old mining area near Rocky Mountain House, Alberta, which was operational until the mid-1950s. Found in a heap on the floor, a rag black from coal dust, it would have been overlooked but for the distinctive brass buttons with the red centres registered by GWG in 1936. Not only are the buttons marked GWG, but the rivets are, too.
Lucie Heins, RAM

Assunta Dotto

Assunta Dotto (née Peron), centre, an Italian immigrant who worked at the factory from 1943 to 1945 and again in the 1960s, said that her father came to Alberta in 1906 at the age of nineteen, intending to bring his family when he had saved enough money. He visited Italy in 1923, returning to Canada when Assunta was eight months old. Due to immigration restrictions, she was sixteen years old when she next saw him in 1939. During World War II, like other Italian immigrants in Alberta, the RCMP fingerprinted her, forced her to register, carry an identification card, and report on a monthly basis. She remembers that, "after a few months, one of the RCMP officials said to me, 'Why are you coming here?' I said, 'Because I was told to come over here.' So he went back in the office and put a stamp on it and said, 'Go and don't come back.'" (LEFT TO RIGHT) Irma Nimis, Assunta Dotto, Juliette Beaudoin. Courtesy of Assunta Dotto

we couldn't go as fast because we had twice as much material to sew you see, and that's what they did. But we all, we all got paid the same amount of money....My godmother said, 'Nelly get smart. When you see the bundles going out, go and get one whether you're finished your other one or not, and put it in your box, and nobody can take it away from you.' So I got smart." In later years, the company paid less per piece for small sizes and more for large sizes, but at this time, they were all rated the same.

At one point during the war, Assunta Dotto (then Peron) remembers that when they were working on shirts for officers in the army the material would bunch up in the machines. The machines had to be adjusted to handle the fine fabric. Although the operators could not work as quickly as usual, they were still paid by the piece. They complained but she said that, because of the war, workers were expected to make sacrifices and no one paid any attention:

> So one day, we were just sitting there waiting for the bell to go after lunch and somebody said, "I think we have a solution here. When the power comes on we'll stop it, maybe they'll listen to us....," Within minutes there was floor ladies, officials, managers, mechanics of course and the union representative....Nobody said anything until they asked us why and we said, "Okay, all we want is to put us on timework until we can pick up speed and then we can go back on piecework because this way we can't even have enough to pay our board." So anyway, they started the machines and between the union and management they came to a deal, whatever they did, we got paid time work for a period of time....But I mean to say we were scared after having done that. It's an understatement. But if we weren't so scared we would have realized that

they couldn't fire us, all of us. Because then they would have come to a total standstill. And after that, we had other problems but never to the extent of turning the power off.

Records of negotiations are contained in the union minutes. When GWG introduced new operations, sometimes the union and management negotiated independently of UGWA headquarters in New York because headquarters would not provide rates. On other occasions, the union sent garments to New York as samples to ask them to set prices for each of the operations. The local was not satisfied with the amount of support that it received from headquarters and did not provide as much money from union dues to headquarters as requested.

The union continued to negotiate for a return to the forty-hour week and paid holidays, also taking this request to the Regional Labor Board, but the board referred it back to management. In the end, this time around, government legislation, rather than negotiations with the union, secured the forty-hour week and paid holidays.

Great Western Garment hired floor women and supervisors from within the plant, often hiring women who had been active within the union and understood the workers' concerns. Great Western Garment, in contrast to other unions, encouraged floor women and floor men to remain in the union, further underlining the cooperation between the union and management.

Dotto recalled that GWG fired her in 1945 because she skipped work to go to the Edmonton Exhibition with a group of her co-workers. She had already given notice that she was quitting to get married and was moving out of town. The girls discussed the idea over lunch in front of the floor lady. Dotto was sitting by the window and saw the streetcar or bus coming and she said, "Come on girls, let's go!" They all took off. When she turned around and saw the floor lady, "she had a look of horror in her face and she was left supposedly to explain why she didn't stop us. But the poor thing, I guess she didn't realize we were serious. So anyway we had a good time and we reported for work the next morning." The supervisor Annie Stephenson and the floor lady Mrs. Nufer were standing at the top of the stairs. "Mrs. Nufer said, 'You, you, you, you in the cafeteria,' and she said, 'I hope you had a good time now you can go back to the exhibition.' She handed us the pay envelope, and I felt horrible — not for me — and I said to her, 'You can't fire me,' I said, 'I've already quit.' But she ignored me. And so, we left and I felt horrible because the other girls had lost their job. But shortly after that I heard that they were all rehired."

Aside from the ongoing challenge of determining a fair rate of pay, Local 120 had a particularly good relationship with Jacox during his long tenure as manager and later president. Even when they disagreed, they were able to discuss issues in a friendly and respectful manner, marked by his attending union meetings to show slides of his trips to Europe and the union giving him an engraved clock for his twentieth anniversary in 1950 in appreciation of his cooperation in improving working conditions, wages, and pensions.

Great Western Garment was the most significant wartime manufacturer in the province, and its president, Clarence Jacox, was named deputy administrator for Alberta for work clothing under the Wartime Prices and Trade Board. The Wartime Prices and Trade Board governed style changes and price ceilings. Great Western Garment kept up with the demands of government contracts but had difficulty buying enough material to fill its orders for work clothes because cotton was required for the military. Consequently, consumers had difficulty finding replacement clothing. There were many shortages and rationed goods during World War II.

A Day in the Life of the Factory

When there were three shifts running, operators worked from midnight to 8:00 a.m., from 8:00 a.m. to 4:00 p.m., or from 4:00 p.m. to midnight.

When the day shift arrived at 8:00 a.m., they punched a time clock. A bell rang to start the day. The workers went to their machines and a bundle girl brought them their work. The floor lady, later instructors, worked with the new girls to show them exactly what they needed to do.

The bell rang at ten o'clock for a fifteen-minute break. Sometimes they oiled their machines during their breaks, but workers were not supposed to touch them until the bell went again to start work. Workers had to provide their own scissors and engraved their names on them so they would not be misplaced or stolen.

At lunchtime, the workers would either go to the GWG cafeteria or to Frank's Café across the street, which was a little quieter. Most workers packed their own lunch and just bought a drink.

The machines were lined up in order, according to the manufacturing process. The bundle boy took the bundles from one worker to the next throughout the day. Each bundle had tickets hanging from it. The operators would remove a ticket and put it in an envelope to hand in to calculate their pay.

Every worker who handled a bundle wrote his or her number on a chart that stayed with the bundle. The examiner inspected completed garments. If the work was not done properly it would come back to be redone on the operator's own time. The hands of those working on denim turned blue from the dye.

Friday, after working a full shift, the tired, hungry, dusty, and sweaty workers lined up to collect their pay envelopes with cash inside, and then paid their union dues to the financial secretary. When they left the factory, the company inspected their bags to make sure they were not taking anything home.

Worth Waiting For

Great Western Garment continued to advertise in farm magazines in order to maintain loyalty among its customers and retailers. GWG provided free Farmers' Almanacs, booklets that people would hang in their kitchens to remind them of GWG throughout the year. Advertisements in the *Country Guide* from 1943 note: "Merchants who are unable to buy stocks of G.W.G. goods, because of scarcity of supply or lack of established quota, should plan to acquire this brand for their stores when peace times return again."

Great Western Garment effectively tied its marketing to the war, building loyalty not just for immediate sales, but also for postwar sales. The company promoted the purchase of well-made clothes as a patriotic act: "Buy only what you need — buy the longest-lasting garments you can get — buy a quality brand." The company acknowledged the critical role of farm families during the war: "All farm families in Western Canada are fighting a tough battle — a battle to increase food production in spite of a shortage of help. As good Canadians they know that to work, to fight, to sacrifice is the price of Victory."

Shortages did not end as soon as the war was over. In 1946 GWG ads noted, "They're still a little scarce, but they're worth waiting for."

Union minutes note that after war ended in Europe, GWG received a contract to produce garments for the forces continuing to fight in the Pacific. Great Western Garment's war-related production was not limited to the Canadian Armed Forces, and did not end immediately when the war ended. The *Edmonton Bulletin*, May 9, 1946, reported, "425 skilled G.W.G. employees busy on government contract: City clothing plant hums with activity supplying garments for Holland's people." The contract was for military uniforms: 68,000 pairs of combination overalls; 15,000 khaki service trousers; 30,000 overalls for the marines; 65,000 flannel shirts; and 35,000 white drill shorts for the air force. Wartime clothing rationing was still in force for Edmonton residents, so the military contract was particularly welcome.

Great Western Garment expanded its plant, upgraded machinery, and increased its workforce significantly during World War II, producing more than $4 million worth of military clothing by 1945 as well as continuing to produce a more limited amount of civilian clothing. When the war was over, GWG had to create a new market for its goods.

✕╌╌╌╌╌╌╌╌╌╌╌╌✕

Cowboy King Jacket, c. 1936-1940s
Although the jacket does not have a brand label, the same style of jacket, with the stitched tucks in front and pleats and cinched back that provide shape and allow mobility, is seen in the GWG catalogues from 1939, identified as a Cowboy King. By 1959 the front featured double lines of topstitching rather than stitched tucks — an easier technique to mass-produce. *GWG Household Handbook, 1942, p. 20. RAM*

"Cowboy King"*
Riding Pants and Jacket

The West's favourite rider suit. Made from special quality 10-oz. "Buckskin" denim. The short jacket is pleated both back and front, and is bar-tacked and stitched with orange thread. Pants have tapered legs, and saddle seat.

No. 516 Blue Pants. Sizes 30 to 44. Price **$2.35**
No. 616 Blue Jackets. Sizes 36 to 46. Price **$2.35**

Registered Trade Mark.

Page 20

GWG on the Home Front

GWG built loyalty among customers by stressing that everyone was making sacrifices and working toward a common goal. A 1944 GWG Christmas card refers to the challenges in providing civilian clothing during wartime and notes, "We shall continue to give you our best attention in the coming year — 1945 — when we hope the world will again know Peace."

Country Guide, June 1943, p. 2. RAM

WORK CLOTHING FOR FIGHTERS ON THE FARM FRONT

All farm families in Western Canada are fighting a tough battle—a battle to increase food production in spite of a shortage of help. As good Canadians they know that to work, to fight, to sacrifice is the price of Victory.

The battle of food production isn't as dangerous or exciting as fighting in the air or on land or on the sea, but it does take plenty of grit and determination to work long hours to produce the food requirements of a nation wholly at war.

As this battle goes on, difficulties and scarcities affect the pro-

duction of everything—even the clothing you wear. Cotton is one of the strategic materials of modern warfare. Requirements of the armed forces come first, so the home front must do with less. See that the work clothing you buy is the best, the longest-lasting you can get.

If you now wear G.W.G. overalls, G.W.G. shirts, G.W.G. pants, or if you can still buy them, remember they are valued possessions, for they are the finest in work clothing. Wear them with care—preserve them, so they'll deliver those extra months of wear built into them.

 THEY WEAR LONGER BECAUSE THEY'RE MADE STRONGER

Merchants who are now unable to buy stocks of G.W.G. goods, because of scarcity of supply or lack of established quota, should plan to acquire this brand for their stores when peace times return again.

Edmonton's own Rosie the Riveter, 1942

As women began working in traditionally male occupations, they began dressing in traditionally male clothing. This catalogue illustration shows women working on aircraft, for which coveralls and slacks were a "necessity." Edmonton's Aircraft Repair Ltd. at Blatchford Field (the municipal airport) was the largest employer of women in the city during the war. Many of the three thousand workers participating in the Commonwealth Air Training Plan were women, including former GWG employee Norah Hook. She left GWG to work for Aircraft Repair Ltd. as the job was less monotonous and allowed more physical mobility.

GWG Household Handbook, 1942, p. 22. RAM

Utility Slacks and Coveralls for Women

All purpose Slacks and Coveralls are necessities for an ever increasing number of women. Many new jobs, new kinds of work require this type of safe and comfortable clothing. Black Twill and Prairie Blue Denim Slacks. Express stripe, Blue "Snobak" denim and White Twill in the Coveralls—Sanforized Shrunk.

No. 279-1	Black Twill Slacks (waist sizes 24 to 32).	Each...................................$1.95
No. 279-25	Blue Denim Slacks (waist sizes 24 to 32).	Each................................... 1.95
No. W 581-3	Express Stripe Coverall (Bust sizes 34 to 44).	Each................................... 3.95
No. W 580	Blue Denim Coverall (Bust sizes 34 to 44).	Each................................... 3.95
No. W 580-2	White Twill Coverall (Bust sizes 34 to 44).	Each................................... 3.95

(Coveralls made short, medium or tall in each size).

Page 22

Prisoner-of-War Uniforms

Great Western Garment manufactured prisoner-of-war uniforms during World War II. In 1941 the federal government issued the first contracts for internees, prisoners-of-war, and refugees. A big red circle was sewn into the back of the jackets, sweaters, and overcoats, and a red stripe about 3″ wide was sewn onto the outside of the trouser seams of POW uniforms. Photograph by Jodi Dolinsky. Red Deer Museum + Art Gallery

Pacific Coast Militia Regiment Battle Dress Drill Blouse, c. 1942

GWG also manufactured uniforms for militia units such as the Pacific Coast Militia Regiment (PCMR). The PCMR was formed early in 1942 in response to the attack on Pearl Harbor, and disbanded following the war. The PCMR recruited men living and working in the area as loggers, trappers, prospectors, and ranchers, who knew the local topography and terrain, to patrol the land along the coast, easing public fears about possible enemy activities. The uniform was introduced after Japan launched fire bombs in Oregon in September 1942. In addition to this battle dress drill blouse, the uniform included pants, a cruiser coat with shoulder straps, shooting hat, steel helmet, and a .303 rifle. Lucie Heins, RAM, H08.17.242

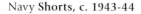

Navy Shorts, c. 1943-44

This Royal Canadian Navy uniform, consisting of white cotton, Naval style shorts and a middy jacket, was manufactured by GWG and issued to Able Seaman W. Pilichowsky, V-49763, 1943-1944. Cutters and machine operators preferred to work on sailors' whites rather than denims because they were easier to handle and there was no dye to transfer to their hands. Lucie Heins, RAM, H01.162.12, 14, 15

Sewing for the Netherlands

The *Edmonton Bulletin* published a series of photographs of workers at the plant in a feature article in 1946 about a large contract that GWG received to produce clothing for the Netherlands. This order was particularly important at a time when the company was still having difficulty securing a consistent supply of material for civilian clothing. PAA, Bl1163.1

A SHORTAGE, YES!

But No Lack of Quality

Remember . . . when you buy work garments that cotton for clothing is scarce. Cotton is vital war material, and war needs must come first. So buy only what you need — buy the longest-lasting garments you can get — buy a quality brand. Quality is the important ingredient . . . whether it be in the rancher's livestock, the farmer's wheat or the work clothes you buy. In the manufacture of G.W.G. work clothes, quality plays a double part, for here you find that good quality material is combined with good quality workmanship.

If you now wear G.W.G. Overalls, G.W.G. Shirts, G.W.G. Pants, or if you can still buy them, remember to wear them with care, conserve the material in them so they'll give you all the extra wear that is built into them. Greater strength in material and construction, greater comfort in fit and style—these contribute more months of wear.

THEY WEAR LONGER BECAUSE THEY'RE MADE STRONGER

Merchants who are now unable to buy stocks of G.W.G. goods, because of scarcity of supply or lack of established quota, should plan to acquire this brand for their stores when peace times return again.

GWG built loyalty among customers by stressing that everyone was making sacrifices and working toward a common goal. GWG acknowledged the critical role of farm families. "All farm families in Western Canada are fighting a tough battle — a battle to increase food production in spite of a shortage of help. As good Canadians they know that to work, to fight, to sacrifice is the price of Victory." *Country Guide*, August 1943, p. 2. RAM.

HOW TO IDENTIFY GWG CLOTHING

Common GWG Logos and Labels

In 1911 the Great Western Garment Company trademarked a logo that showed the interlocking letters "GWG" in front of a circle, with eagle wings extending from the tips of the "W." A similar logo was registered in 1912 but does not appear to have been widely used, if at all, and that trademark has since been erased. GWG trademarked the famous red dot behind its initials in 1929.

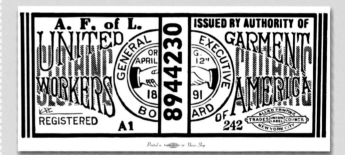

UGWA label, 1950s. Early garments have both a GWG label and a United Garment Workers of America union label, purchased by Local 120 from UCWA headquarters in New York and hand-sewn into garments made by unionized workers. Variations of the UGWA label with red ink were used before the 1950s, and those marked CIO later. RAM

1. Sanforized Shrunk, from GWG Catalogue 1939. Garments of the period were labelled Sanforized Shrunk or Unshrunk. RAM

2. In 1953 GWG labels featured the original logo with black or navy blue letters in front of a red circle, the words "union made," and either a ® or the words "registered trade mark." Lucie Heins, RAM, H08.17.56

3. Filed in 1964 and registered in 1965, a modernized logo rendered the initials "GWG" in a sans serif font, and two straight lines extending from the "W" replaced the feathered wings. Lucie Heins, RAM, H08.17.50

4. A stylized "GWG" logo with a circle behind the "W" was filed in 1971 and registered the next year. From 1972 to 1974, GWG used a modified version of this logo, with the letters "GWG" in blue over a red circle with a blue outline. Lucie Heins, RAM, H08.17.11

5. This logo, with a capital "G," a small "w," and a capital "G" inset on the diagonal into a square, was filed in 1981 and registered in 1982. Lucie Heins, RAM, H08.17.24

6. When GWG celebrated its seventy-fifth anniversary in 1986, it introduced retro advertising. This Great Western Garment Company logo, filed in 1989 and registered in 1990, incorporates the full original company name. A similar logo, but without the words "Great Western Garment Company," was introduced in 1991. Lucie Heins, RAM, H08.17.39

Buttons, Zippers, and Rivets

Zippers were used on GWG garments from the 1930s on, though Cowboy King pants had a button fly until 1963. Rust-proof, nickel Lightning zippers are mentioned by name in the 1963 and 1965 catalogues.

1 Trouser button, c. 1911-1915. Lucie Heins, RAM, H08.78.1

2 In use since 1934 and registered 1936, rust-proof brass buttons marked "G.W.G. REG." with a red dot in the centre. Lucie Heins, RAM, H08.17.119

3 From 1953 to 1963, bright brass buttons marked "G.W.G. REG." Lucie Heins, RAM, H08.17.43.

4 From 1963 to 1972 dull bronze buttons marked "G.W.G. REG." Lucie Heins, RAM, H08.17.42

5 From 1964 to 1972 brass buttons marked "Kings." Lucie Heins, RAM, H08.17.60

6 From 1972 to 1982, brass buttons and snaps with a pattern that mimics the back pocket stitching. Lucie Heins, RAM, H08.17.36

7 From 1972 to 1974, brass buttons with a stylized "GWG." Lucie Heins, RAM, H08.17.50

8 Copper rivets with the initials "GWG" on them were used on the crotch and pockets of Cowboy King jeans until the early 1960s and again on GWGs in the 1980s. Lucie Heins, RAM, H08.17.17

4

5

8

7

6

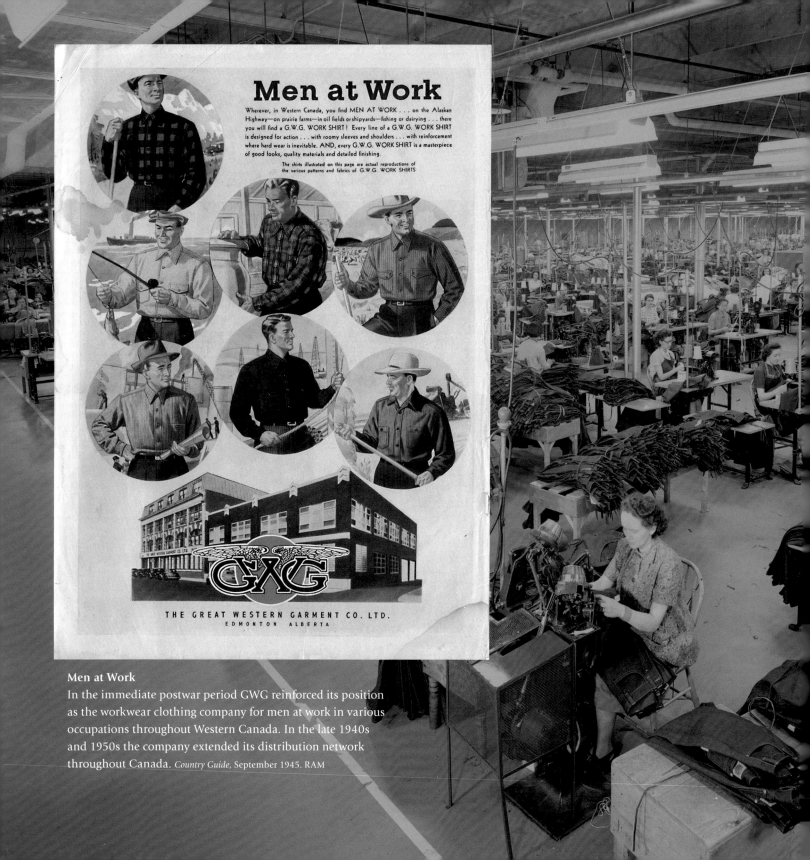

Men at Work

Wherever, in Western Canada, you find MEN AT WORK . . . on the Alaskan Highway—on prairie farms—in oil fields or shipyards—fishing or dairying . . . there you will find a G.W.G. WORK SHIRT! Every line of a G.W.G. WORK SHIRT is designed for action . . . with roomy sleeves and shoulders . . . with reinforcement where hard wear is inevitable. AND, every G.W.G. WORK SHIRT is a masterpiece of good looks, quality materials and detailed finishing.

The shirts illustrated on this page are actual reproductions of the various patterns and fabrics of G.W.G. WORK SHIRTS

GWG

THE GREAT WESTERN GARMENT CO. LTD.
EDMONTON ALBERTA

Men at Work
In the immediate postwar period GWG reinforced its position as the workwear clothing company for men at work in various occupations throughout Western Canada. In the late 1940s and 1950s the company extended its distribution network throughout Canada. *Country Guide*, September 1945. RAM

CHAPTER FOUR

THERE WERE A NUMBER OF SIGNIFICANT changes at Great Western Garment in the postwar period. GWG had increased its capacity in order to meet wartime demands. After the war, in order to stay profitable, the company expanded its product line beyond workwear and a small range of sportswear to casual clothing for the entire family, and spread its sales and distribution network beyond Western Canada across the country.

However, material shortages continued to cause work disruptions. Often orders had to be cancelled and production shifted to different garments when materials were not received on time. Each type of garment and each type of fabric required a different set-up of the sewing machines. Something as small as replacing a button when the buttons normally used were unavailable required the union and management to discuss whether different pay rates were required.

Workers were periodically granted a set minimum wage until the rates for new machinery, styles, and fabrics could be determined. GWG sometimes offered "goods money" in addition to the amount per operation, if the fabric was particularly heavy or difficult to work with. If GWG could not move workers to other lines when there were surpluses of finished goods, GWG laid them off for days or weeks until there was work for them.

In 1946 GWG restored the forty-hour workweek. The provincial government introduced more workers' benefits. The government set statutory holidays for its own employees that were a guideline for private industry. The union negotiated with management for paid statutory holidays and paid vacation time. The plant closed for two weeks for summer vacation, as was common practice in factories. It would have been too difficult for operators to choose their own holiday times because each line worked as a team.

The Alberta Blue Cross Plan was introduced in 1948 to provide affordable coverage for hospital services for working-class Albertans. Shortly after, the union entered into a group plan, allowing workers to opt in or out. Workers who required hospitalization appreciated the plan. Within months, the union received a note expressing the gratitude of a worker who had to pay only $15 of a $195 hospitalization bill. She could not have afforded to pay the full amount.

According to union minutes, wages continued to be the major issue between the union and management. In 1947 the union again requested an increase in wages, but Jacox pointed out that if the firm were to give workers an increase in wages, they would have to increase the price of garments by fifty or sixty cents, making the company vulnerable to competition from manufacturers in Winnipeg. When the union requested an increase in 1949, Jacox countered that workers' earnings had increased 250 percent since 1939, that the increase in cost of living was significantly lower in Edmonton than the national average, and that workers' wages

REQUIRE

**WOMEN
SEWING MACHINE
OPERATORS**

for

**ALL ELECTRIC
EQUIPMENT**

• • •

Experience Not
Necessary

**Permanent Work
At Good Wages**

Excellent working condition in one of Canada's most modern factories. Employees enjoy a 5-day week—cafeteria privileges —and company nursing services.
Apply in person Monday thru Friday at 2 p.m., or write

THE
**GREAT WESTERN
GARMENT CO.**
Edmonton — Limited

Women's "Cowboy King" RIDER PANTS

"Cowboy King" Rider Pants specially styled for women in "Snobak" ® denim. Their good looks and outstanding quality make them ideal for all outdoor wear either for work or sport. Side opening fastening. Sanforized shrunk.

Women's sizes 24 to 32

$3.95

Girls' sizes 6 to 12 years

$3.25

W-516

Women at Play

GWG began to develop clothing for women based upon the styles that were popular for men. One of the first styles introduced for women was Cowboy King rider jeans; they were styled for women but the brand name was already very familiar. GWG Catalogue, 1950, p. 37. RAM

FACING PAGE:

Hiring Sewing Operators

The workforce grew significantly in the postwar period, and there was always a lot of turnover within the plant. GWG periodically ran advertisements in local newspapers looking for machine operators. They continued to advertise the five-day week, cafeteria and nursing privileges that made GWG a good place to work. *Edmonton Bulletin,* May 8, 1948.

A Modern Factory on 86 Street and 106 A Avenue

The new factory, a reinforced concrete and masonry structure designed by architect Ralph Brownlee, was the largest garment factory on the continent. In 1954 GWG sold the building to Great-West Life Assurance and signed a twenty-year lease to free up capital for further business expansion. PAA, J181.1

Opening Celebrations

In 1953 GWG chose an unusual location for its Christmas party. Where soon sewing machines would be lined up, staff in their festive clothes enjoyed the buffet and ate together at tables on the factory floor as GWG celebrated the completion of its new factory on December 18, 1953. PAA, Bl2143

Recognition for Long-term Employees
In 1948, at the request of the union, Jacox recognized the contributions of long-term employees at the union-management banquet. The banquet was an annual tradition for many years. Paid for by both the union and management, it was a rare opportunity for the workers to socialize among themselves and with those working in other aspects of the company. Local 120 Collection. PAA

would increase through the introduction of new equipment and procedures. The union accepted his arguments.

The annual union-management banquet was the primary social outlet for workers. In 1950 the workers organized boys' fastball and girls' softball teams outfitted with uniforms from GWG, and in 1954, curling teams with trophies provided by GWG. Few workers remember participating in any social activities outside of the plant.

Great Western Garment expanded beyond the 97 Street plant and in the early 1950s began to look for a site to construct a new factory. Planning and construction took two years. GWG was so frustrated by its negotiations with the city over potential sites that Jacox suggested he was considering moving the factory to Central Canada.

GWG searched for a location near the existing plant. They wanted to remain close to the homes of workers in the inner city, to accommodate their need to juggle work and domestic duties. In 1952 GWG purchased a 1.3-hectare site at 86 Street and 106A Avenue, near Clarke Stadium. The stadium site had been zoned for a school. Area residents protested rezoning the property to allow the factory to be constructed. They argued that the factory would reduce property values in what was, at the time, a respectable residential area. Carl Berg, representing the Boyle Street Community League, supported GWG's request and the company agreed to maintain an existing playground for area children. Over the years, property values did decline in the area.

When GWG vacated the old factory on 97 Street, the building reverted to its original use as a department store and became the north-side location for the Army & Navy Department Stores.

On December 18, 1953, just a few months behind schedule,

Ranch Boss, 1959
Ranch Boss Western style pants and jackets were similar to the Cowboy King brand, but never as popular.
Lucie Heins, RAM, H08.17.131

the firm celebrated the completion of the new factory—a one-storey, 9,290-square metre plant with a 6,500-square metre sewing room. Students from schools in Edmonton and surrounding towns visited Edmonton's two most important landmarks, the GWG factory and the Alberta Legislature Building. People who grew up in nearby towns remember this as a highlight of their school years.

Garment manufacturers came from around the world to see the new plant, the largest in North America. They were impressed with the size of the plant and its highly engineered, efficient production process. GWG acquired specialized, automated machinery as soon as it became available. Most machinery was less than three years old and the company expected to increase production by 20 percent, even before increasing the number of employees from 500 to 750.

As well as increasing the number of workers by 50 percent, "speed up" was constant. Operations were broken down into many steps over the years. Time engineers watched the operators and showed them how to expend less energy using particular motions, how to pick the pieces up, which fingers to use, and how to feed fabric into the machine. The union and management would set a rate. Once the operators became proficient, they changed the construction methods a little bit and set a higher rate.

Anne Ozipko remembered, "One time the engineer was standing behind me, and I turned around and said to him, 'Do you need a whip?'" The time engineers were supposed to set the rates based upon the work of an average worker, but they would set the rate based upon the work of the fastest operator. Where possible, operations were fully automated and the operators simply placed the fabric pieces in the correct position. Ozipko said that two of the engineers had "engineered soup cans in England. What do they know about sewing anyway?"

Even though the plant was situated as close as possible to the old factory, workers complained about poor bus service so the company approached the city to improve service. Eileen Hatch, who worked in the office from 1953 to 1958, remembered that she used to let the transit department know when operators would be working on a holiday to ensure that there were buses available. Great Western Garment was now one of Alberta's largest industrial enterprises. Yet it continued to expand. In 1957 GWG built an 11,610-square metre addition to the new factory, further increasing the size of its workforce.

See Canada First!
enjoy the wonders of your own country in...

G.W.G. Garments

The Finest
Garments
Made Anywhere!

Illustrated on this page

Men's *"TEXAS RANGER" Matched Outfits

Ladies' *"FRONTIER QUEEN" Matched Outfits

Boys' and Girls' *"COWBOY KING" Rider Pants

UNION LABEL

GWG

*REG.

*G.W.G. BRAND NAMES
ARE REGISTERED
TRADE MARKS

Most admired and most desired!

For comfortable smart summer wear . . . . .
there's a G.W.G. garment for every occasion. Look
for the famous G.W.G. winged label on the
garment— your assurance of quality — always!

At leading stores across Canada

Made in Canada's Most Modern Garment Factory by

THE GREAT WESTERN GARMENT CO. LTD., EDMONTON

Star Weekly, Toronto, June 14, 1958

DOUG STEPHENS, 1918–1972

Doug Stephens grew up in the Old West: homesteading, working as a ranch hand and rodeo competitor. He served in the RCAF during World War II. Following the war, he studied art in England and under Norman Rockwell at the Art Centre School in Los Angeles. Stephens became the commercial art director for Commonwealth Printing in Calgary. His signature appears on many GWG advertisements in the mid- to late-1950s published in national magazines and in GWG catalogues. Stephens was known as Calgary's original Cowboy Artist, and while some ads had a Western or cowboy theme, others reflected idealized families throughout Canada. *Star Weekly,* June 14, 1958, RAM

Driller's Drill, 1948

Great Western Garment introduced Driller's Drill clothing in 1948 following the discovery of oil at Leduc, Alberta, in 1947, demonstrating that GWG was still strongly aligning its destiny with Alberta's. The brand name was a play on words, the drill referring to both the driller's tool and the strong diagonal weave of the fabric. A 1954 ad in the *Star Weekly* announced that the new fabric was the result of three years of research to develop a more durable fabric. This glass slide was an advertisement used in movie theatres at the time.

PAA, 73.308.105

Frisco Jeans, 1949
First introduced as a black jean in 10-oz denim, Frisco Jeans later became one of GWG's matched sets. This is the only ad located to date that uses film stars to promote GWGs. GWG photographed Valerie Allen and Peter Baldwin at Paramount Studios in Hollywood. Allen appeared in *Hot Spell* (1958) and Baldwin in *The Trap* (1959), but neither was a headlining star, and their connection to Alberta or GWG is unknown.
Maclean's, October 11, 1958, RAM

Ranch Style Garments

515-22 MEN'S "RANCH BOSS" WESTERN STYLE RIDER PANTS Black. Waist sizes 28 to 42. Leg lengths 28 to 36 — **5 95**

515-15 As above, in suntan shade — **5 95**

220-15 MEN'S "DRILLERS' DRILL" JACKETS Suntan shade. Sizes 36 to 50 — **6 95**

220-20 As above in Black — **6 95**

MEN'S *"SPRINGBOK"* MATCHED SETS

69 2 MEN'S "SPRINGBOK" SATEEN TWILL PANTS, to match "Husky" Shirts. Suntan shade. Sizes 30 to 44 — **6 95**

69 1 As above, in green — **6 95**

69 3 As above, in grey — **6 95**

69 12 As above, in charcoal — **6 95**

133 92 MEN'S SATEEN TWILL SUMMER WEIGHT "HUSKY" SHIRT to match "Springbok" pants. Suntan shade. Sizes 14½ to 17½ — **4 95**

133 91 As above, in green — **4 95**

133 93 As above, in grey — **4 95**

133 96 As above, in charcoal — **4 95**

Springbok and Ranch Boss, 1959
GWG designed Men's Springbok sateen twill pants to wear with Husky shirts as a "matched set." The combination could easily be adapted for use as a tradesman's uniform, an outfit that looked more professional than jeans or overalls but did not require dry cleaning like a suit so was more appropriate for work outside an office. GWG Catalogue, 1959, p. 7. RAM

1953 Logo
The logo remained largely unchanged through the 1950s; although, the words "Sanforized Shrunk" and/or "Union Made" sometimes appeared with the logo. In 1953 GWG labels featured the original logo with black or navy blue letters in front of a red circle, the words "Union Made," and either a ® or the words "Registered Trade Mark." GWG Catalogue, 1959 p. 2. RAM

Frontier Queen, 1959
GWG gave the Frontier Queen brand to Western-style slacks designed for women with waist sizes 24″ to 34″ in short, medium, and long lengths. Advertisements for Frontier Queen slacks showed pictures of various fabric swatch choices. *Maclean's* and the *Star Weekly*, as well as the *1959* GWG Catalogue, featured this advertisement.

Maclean's, April 11, 1959, RAM

"Featured at Leading Stores across Canada"

Great Western Garment began to change its marketing strategy, advertising in mainstream national magazines as well as in agricultural media. Great Western Garment advertisements appeared regularly on the inside back cover of *Maclean's*, "Canada's National Magazine," and in the *Star Weekly*, Toronto's weekend magazine. The company introduced the slogan: "Featured at Leading Stores across Canada." GWGs were now available from coast to coast—six thousand retailers carried GWG clothing. Like GWG, Levis Strauss, which began in San Francisco, expanded into the eastern United States in the 1950s. Levi's® became popular with American celebrities and youth.

Advertisements showed the entire family wearing the popular GWG brands, some of which came in matched outfits. GWG manufactured women's clothing in a range of fabrics, bright colours, stripes, and checks. In the *Star Weekly*, July 5, 1958, GWG claimed, "There's a G.W.G. garment for every member of the family that's right for every occasion—tough and rugged for outdoor work or play—smart and comfortable for fun and relaxation." GWG sized its children's clothing by age, and men's and women's in tall, medium, and short. In addition to the familiar images of workers, farmers, and cowboys, the postwar advertisements focus on mum, dad, and the kids planning and enjoying their summer holidays, sightseeing in the mountains, relaxing in the great outdoors, picnicking, barbecuing, or heading off to school or college. New brands introduced included: Driller's Drill (1948), Frisco Jeans (1949), High Rigger (1951), Frontier Queen (1959), Springbok (1959), Strapback (1959), and Ranch Boss (1959).

Workers on the Move

With the discovery of oil in Leduc, Edmonton entered a period of prosperity and other employment options became available to Canadian women. According to the municipal census, in the fifteen years after the war, Edmonton's population more than doubled from 111,745 in 1945 to 276,018 by 1961.

Canadian immigration restrictions relaxed in 1947, and the workforce at GWG became increasingly diverse as Europeans immigrated to Edmonton. Almost 250,000 displaced persons came to Canada from refugee camps in Europe, many of them to Alberta, in the five years between 1947 and 1952.

International events such as the Hungarian revolution of 1956 continued to drive immigration in this period. Many immigrant women ended up at GWG. Those who were well-educated professionals often had difficulty getting work in their fields, particularly if their English was limited and professional accreditations were not recognized.

Some immigrants, the Germans and Dutch for example, assimilated quickly so they were less readily identified as immigrants within the workforce at GWG. Their co-workers sometimes perceived others, such as the Ukrainians and Poles or Italians and Portuguese, as being from the same countries. In the immediate postwar period, workers felt some of the European tensions within the plant and there were occasionally fights among workers. Union minutes noted incidents of theft of clothing and other personal items for the first time. One former worker remembered "scissors flying" once.

As well as the European immigrants, there was an influx of people from the rural areas around Edmonton into the city. Machinist Max Bedard remembered GWG encouraging Ukrainian settlers to move to Edmonton to work in the factory. There were few opportunities for employment, marriage and personal growth, for younger children in large farm families, and little education available to them in small towns.

Mary Romanuk was one of fifteen children of Polish/Ukrainian immigrants raised in Myrnam. She moved to Edmonton after she married in 1951. "No money, and so only jobs that were available was GWG for inexperienced, twenty-one-year-old girl with no education, except [grade] twelve—didn't mean anything, even in those days. So GWG was the only job I could get." She began working as an operator and later became a supervisor, staying until 1978.

Similarly, Anne Baranyk (now Broad) was born in Calgary, raised on a farm near Elk Point, and moved to the city in 1952. She began working at GWG in 1954 as an examiner. She spoke English well, had taken correspondence studies, and became president of the union.

Canadian women spoke about the strong work ethic of the immigrant women employed at the plant. Mary Romanuk remembers how hard-working the immigrant women were: "Italians, Portuguese, Hungarians, where they also had hard life, and they would try and get every cent they could. So, a lot of them would want to work through the lunch hour if they could, just to make extra money.…And of course the union would say, 'No, you've to stop at 12:00.'" The European workers were so appreciative of the work that, Romanuk remembers, GWG management had to stop them from giving the supervisors Christmas presents.

> Here these people are working hard, and they want
> to maybe gain favours or whatever. They present
> me with statues, with gifts of clothing and oh,
> all kinds of gifts, glassware, ornaments…toasters.
> I had a griddle, a waffle iron, all kinds of presents,
> because they were so appreciative to have a job,
> and to work, and to be able to work, and, and

"NWT" Collectors' Shorthand for "New, With Tags"
Most vintage GWG clothing that has been preserved is unsold stock that was acquired from general stores and clothing stores that put garments away in the attic or basement when they went out of style. Vintage clothing is fashionable again. Clothing that did not sell in the 1950s, 1960s, and 1970s is collectable today. Often it was the unusual sizes that did not sell: garments that were either very small…or very large. For collectors, mint condition, never-worn clothing complete with labels may or may not be more valuable than used clothing, depending upon whether or not they intend to wear it. Driller's Drill pants, Lucie Heins, RAM, H08.17.57

be appreciated. So they were very well liked and they did a good job, and European people worked harder, I think sometimes, I'm sorry to say, than Canadians because we had easier life here. Some.

Eileen Hatch, a Canadian-born woman who worked in the office from 1952 to 1958, also noted the relationship between operators and supervisors. She mentioned that the factory was "Little Germany and Little Italy, whoever happened to be the head supervisor." Ilene Yeandle, the nurse at the plant from 1956 to 1984, said that when she started, "the employees at the time were mostly German, Ukrainian, and some Italian. Then, during the time that I was there, there was this bad

A Field Trip to the GWG Factory
Mini Red Strap overalls and Cowboy King jeans were given to girls who toured the GWG plant and as essay writing prizes. The union also exhibited them in trade fair displays. It has been suggested that they were used as salesmen's samples and that operators made them when learning how to perform various operations, although none of the former salesmen or operators interviewed remember using or making them. Salesmen's samples are usually more accurate. Close examination reveals that the pockets and fly on the jeans are false, so it is unlikely that they were used for this purpose.
Lucie Heins, RAM, H08.17.195

Carpenters' Overalls and Truckers' Leg Aprons

Great Western Garment produced a number of garments designed to be worn by men working in specific trades. The Journeyman Carpenters' overalls and truckers' leg aprons are two examples. They were made of heavy fabric, with reinforced stitching, pockets, and hammer loops. GWG Catalogue, 1950, p. 9. RAM

513

JOURNEYMAN CARPENTER

513—G.W.G. Truckers' Leg Apron
Heavy duty khaki duck—metal rings and tie strap fastener—7 roomy pockets—2 hammer loops—leather reinforced crotch—strong double stitched seams. Sizes small, medium, large $2.95

526—G.W.G. Carpenters' Overall
Extra heavy white duck with every facility for the carpenter. 12 pockets—five section swing-free nail apron—double knees—hammer and axe loops—double and triple stitched—stapled buttons. Sizes 32 to 50 $5.25

Sport Togs, 1950

GWG used the Sport Togs label on wool flannel shirts. The style was a combination of a shirt and a jacket. It could be worn alone as a shirt or over another shirt as a jacket. The style became known as the Jackshirt, in red the quintessential Canadian hunting jacket. First used in 1939, GWG discontinued the brand during the war, reintroduced it in 1950, and Sport Togs remained popular throughout the 1950s.
GWG Catalogue, 1950, p. 42. RAM

Sport Togs PURE WOOL

W-128-41

W-128-39

W-128-40

Men's Virgin Wool Shirts
A smart looking G.W.G. sport shirt tailored from 17 ounce virgin wool shirting that means real warmth with-out weight. Made in jacket style, it can be worn in or out as preferred. Full cut for extra comfort—2 button-down breast pockets—new patterns and shades as shown.
Sizes 14½ to 17½ $7.25

Page 42

Diverse Workplace

Before and during World War II, most workers at GWG were English-speaking. Some were of Scandinavian or Ukrainian descent, children of farmers from the surrounding region. Italians began working at the plant during and after the war. In the 1950s many displaced Europeans started working at the plant. Immigrants came to build a new future for themselves, and particularly for their children. PAA, 1968, BI2157.1

Language Became an Issue

As the workforce became more multilingual, notices were frequently distributed in more than one language, initially Ukrainian in the 1950s, but more recently Chinese or Punjabi. In 1953, when the union was considering introducing a medical insurance plan, the floor lady, Mrs. Nufer, was asked to explain it to the workers in their own languages. However, workers were discouraged from speaking any language but English at work. *Edmonton Journal, 1968, J181.2*

uprising in Hungary, and we had a lot of applicants from Hungary at that time."

Although many Hungarian immigrants came from professional backgrounds, they often had to work as labourers, Elizabeth Kozma and her husband among them. They arrived with two small children in Halifax in January 1957 and took the train to Edmonton. One of her husband's relatives recommended that she approach GWG. People told her that "lots of people come to work there…who didn't speak the language." She had been to technical school and worked in time engineering in a factory in Hungary. At GWG, she began as an operator, topstitching pockets and attaching waistbands. Eventually she became a supervisor and grew to appreciate her work at GWG and later Levi Strauss, but in the beginning she stayed because, "I had to stay there, I have two children…we need the money you know." She said that a number of Hungarian workers came to work at the plant but most did not stay for very long. As Kozma put it, "Well, not every, everybody like hard work." Those that did stay were worried about their relatives in Hungary and supported one another through a difficult time.

Industrial Nursing

Ilene Yeandle, the plant nurse, was initially also responsible for hiring operators. She said that immigrant women would often come to the plant with a relative or someone from their church to translate for them during the hiring interview. She performed a vision test and filled out a medical questionnaire, asking the women about their previous work experience and family situation. New employees were tested for venereal disease, and due to another outbreak of tuberculosis, all employees were again given X-rays on site. GWG had a Red Cross blood donor clinic on site in the late 1950s and provided polio vaccines at a good price.

The introduction of new fabrics, dyes, chemical finishes, and production methods sometimes caused concerns in terms of off-gassing, lint, heat, and other discomforts. Each operation left the workers vulnerable to different problems. Women who worked on the tacking machine sometimes tacked their fingers. Occasionally workers cut themselves with scissors and had to go to the hospital for stitches.

Nurse Yeandle did not recall many serious injuries during her time at the plant. The most serious was when a woman who was putting rivets in the coveralls

> …put a rivet in her thumb. Her supervisor brought her into my office carrying this great big pair of coveralls, and her thumb riveted to the coveralls. I thought this is going to look funny going to hospital, dragging these coveralls with me. The supervisor took her scissors and just cut around it. So I went to hospital with the employee. We went into emergency and they came and announced they may have to amputate her thumb. I thought, oh I hope not. But they were able to remove it, thank goodness. Another time a lady…got her hand caught in the conveyor belt. She took some ends of her fingers off.

Other long-term health conditions may have started during that time but not been recognized by the employees or the nurse. For the women working on sergers that sewed and cut the fabric simultaneously, it was particularly dusty. Anne Ozipko mentioned that she opened up her wristwatch "one time and it was full of lint in there, just packed."

Lillian Wasylynchuk, who died in 2009, was convinced that working at the plant from 1956 to 1963 had caused her chronic lung condition. One of the doctors she consulted observed, "Your lung tissue is not a healthy tissue, it's a denim blue colour. That's the first thing that hit me. The dyes, the dust from the denim jean fabric. At that time, the denims were very hard like fibreglass. When it went through the serger you had a lot of dust. I never realized that this was going to hurt me that bad." She commented about friends at the plant also suffering from emphysema and other conditions. Few wore masks at the time.

Some operators developed long-term conditions such as carpal tunnel syndrome or tendonitis from the repetitive motions. Some developed rotator cuff problems from throwing heavy bundles of partially finished garments into the bundle box. The instructors and time engineers were responsible for showing the operators how to work most efficiently without injury. They were given adjustable chairs to reduce back and shoulder problems. Operators working on particularly noisy machines, such as the machine that put on snaps, were given earplugs. In the early years, when most of the workers lived near the plant, the nurse made house calls to follow up on workers with longer illnesses or conditions. But as the city grew that became impossible.

If asked, the nurse also provided one-on-one advice during pregnancy. No one ever gave birth at work, but Yeandle said, "It's a wonder, because they would work right as close as they possibly could." In 1959 the union lobbied for women to retain their seniority when they had a baby. They had to leave work from the time they were six months pregnant and were given a leave of absence for five to six months, but had to return to work when the baby was only three months old in order to keep a job, not necessarily on their former machine. They received no financial compensation.

EMILY ROSS, UNION ACTIVIST

Emily Bullock was born in Yorkshire, England, in 1899 and worked as a spinner and weaver from the age of fourteen before immigrating to Alberta to join her sister, a war bride, in 1920. In 1922 she began working for GWG as an operator. She married Tony Ross in 1926 and left work to have her son Jack a year later.

She returned to GWG c. 1932 and became involved in the union as recording secretary, and in 1943 she became president of Local 120 and UGWA organizer for Western Canada. She soon left GWG because of the amount of travel required of a union organizer.

She assisted the union in its negotiations with management concerning wages, working conditions, the introduction of new piecework systems, and grievances, and promoted the use of the union label and solidarity with other unions.

She was a delegate to the ETLC from 1940 to 1955 and advised Local 120 to work through the ETLC and the AFL to demand improvements to provincial labour legislation. She represented the local at AFL and CTLC conventions, accompanied UGWA representatives on visits to Canadian locals, and represented Canadian workers at the British Trade Union Congress several times in the early 1950s.

In 1954 she became a member of the UGWA General Executive in New York and was the only female international representative of the American Federation of Labor in Canada.

The ETLC Labor Day Annual said: "She deplores the lack of women in the labor movement and is firm in her belief that women should serve as officers of their local unions and attend trades and labor council meetings."

She and her husband moved to Vancouver in 1956 to join their son, but she remained active within UGWA and continued to be influential in Local 120's contract negotiations through the 1960s.

Emily Ross died in Vancouver in 1980.

UGWA publication, Local 120 Collection. PAA

Mrs. Mooney and Local 120 Executive Members, June 1956
The visit of Marie Mooney from the Pricing Department in New York in 1956
underlined the fact that the Edmonton union operated quite independently of UGWA
headquarters. Mooney said that she was pleased to see the prices were as good as they
were. She noted that it had been more than twenty years since UGWA had checked
the prices but at the same time spoke to union members about the benefits the local
received through UGWA. Photograph by Laddie Ponich, Local 120 Collection. PAA

Challenges Ahead

In 1958 C.D. Jacox died and was succeeded by J. Gerald Godsoe of Toronto. Godsoe was very conservative. The relationship between Godsoe and the union, which was led by Anne Baranyk from 1956 to 1970, was more difficult than it had been under Jacox. Jacox's death precipitated not only a change in management, but within a few years, a change in ownership.

At the same time that the company was expanding, it was also being subjected to its first real threat from globalization. GWG could meet competition from non-unionized Canadian firms by improving efficiencies in the plant and producing better quality goods, but in the postwar period, GWG, like other Canadian garment manufacturers, began to be impacted by competition from non-unionized manufacturers in Asia. The cost of production in Canada was significantly higher than in Asia, where newly industrialized countries began to challenge the dominance of advanced industrial nations.

As early as 1950, union minutes note their protest to the federal government against the import of inexpensive Japanese goods: "Cheap Japanese shirts and sports clothing has been entering Canada and selling in Canadian stores for ridiculously low prices thus making it more difficult to sell the garments which we make for Union wages. An investigation showed that labourers who manufactured this cheap clothing were paid thirty cents per day. No Canadian will work for such wages, especially us who are union organized."

In 1957 the union again demanded action from the federal government to put Japanese clothing imports on a more competitive basis. However, the government did not support their requests. Management used this competition with imported goods as an argument against increasing wages. Rather than fighting for an increase as UGWA International Organizer Emily Ross had at the end of the war, Ross asked workers to cooperate with management, "stating that we are fortunate to have steady employment in view of the Japanese competition, and lower paid factories in Canada."

In 1961, GWG's fiftieth anniversary, the union proposed a resolution at the AFL to protect clothing manufacturing trades from foreign imports. At the same time, the company itself was bought by an American firm. Levi Strauss & Co. (LS&CO.) of California bought 75 percent of the GWG Company. Owners Peter and Walter Haas joined the board, but GWG retained independent management until after the company's seventy-fifth anniversary in 1986.

ANNE BARANYK, PRESIDENT OF LOCAL 120 UGWA, 1956-1970

Anne Baranyk (now Broad) was born in Calgary, raised on a farm near Elk Point, and moved to Edmonton in 1952. She began working at GWG in quality control as an examiner in 1954, and soon became involved with the union.

From her first day, she was surprised to meet people who thought they had to be careful about what they said at work. Their jobs were very important to them, and they were afraid to raise even minor complaints. She became their spokesperson.

She joined the Grievance Committee, negotiating numerous grievances, large and small, on behalf of the workers. Then she became label secretary, keeping track of the labels purchased from UGWA and sewn into GWG garments. She attended her first AFL Convention and went to the labour school in Banff in 1954 and the TLC Congress in Windsor, Ontario, the following year.

In 1956 former president Louis Kabesh encouraged her to run for president of Local 120, a position she held for fourteen years. Kabesh remained on the board as secretary. Baranyk was bilingual (English and Ukrainian), had studied business through correspondence school, and became a strong negotiator.

She negotiated piecework rates and hourly wages when GWG introduced new machines or product lines. She went to UGWA headquarters in New York to get support for workers concerned about speed-up. She ensured that injured workers received compensation and retained their positions at the plant when they returned to work. She requested that management analyze fabrics that off-gassed to ensure they were not harmful to the workers.

Baranyk left the plant in 1970 and became the agent for the union. She was president of the Edmonton and District Labour Council from 1974 to 1978 prior to her marriage to labour activist Bill Broad and subsequent retirement. Local 120 Collection. PAA

High Rigger, 1951

High Rigger jeans, made of Buckskin denim, were referred to in ads of the early 1950s that listed various GWG brands but soon disappeared. Named for the worker whose job in a lumber camp was to climb very high trees with spurs strapped to his legs and a steel coiled rope, to chop the branches as he climbed, and at the sixty-centimetre diameter mark — thirty to sixty metres in the air — to take off the top of the tree with an axe and a small filing saw. The High Rigger brand was another effort to associate a particular garment with a particular occupation. Courtesy of Ian McDonald

FACING PAGE: **Canadian Trades and Labour Congress (CTLC) Promoted Union Made Goods**

In 1954 the Union Label Trades Department of the CTLC organized a display of union label goods at its convention in Regina. Emily Ross (right), vice-president of the Union Label Trades Department and the Western Canada Organizer for UGWA, worked with Local 120 president Louis Kabesh (left) and auditor Kay Popowich (centre) to create this display. Union labels had to be purchased from UGWA in New York and were expensive because of the duty charged by the federal government. Canadian locals argued that the UGWA should allow them to print the labels in Canada but UGWA disagreed. In the early 1960s GWG discontinued use of a separate union label. Photograph by Heenan, Regina, Local 120 Collection. PAA

THE LAST BEST WEST

The Great Western Garment Company associated itself with the prevalent notion of the Canadian West as the last frontier. Initially "Made in the West for the West," GWG built its reputation on making strong hardwearing clothing for the strong, hard-working men who settled the West. Advertisements featured romantic illustrations that showed idealized men conquering a forbidding land.

The GWG man was handsome, brave, and adventurous. He visually dominated mountains, forests, and the Canadian winter. He was comfortable and confident in the most inaccessible environments. In one advertisement, beams of light through the trees lend him an almost god-like aura. He handled his work with ease, using powerful tools to take control of his environment, while his glance or lifted hand led the viewer's eye to GWG's winged logo. Although he was shown in a rugged landscape, the GWG man was not rough. His clothing, like the man himself, stood up to the elements and yet remained clean and neatly pressed.

By incorporating the frontier concept into their marketing campaigns, GWG was continuing a long tradition of depicting the West as a frontier landscape. It was an effective strategy. Western, rural consumers identified with the imagery, which also reinforced urban, Eastern Canadians' views of the West. Most importantly, the qualities of strength, power, and integrity demonstrated by the men on the land and in the air were qualities with which GWG wanted to be associated.

GWG Catalogue, 1938, p. 16. RAM

Giant New Fairchild at Cooking Lake, Alberta

Pilots who fly giant modern airplanes down north, in all kinds of winter weather, to the famous new mining towns of Goldfields, in northern Saskatchewan, Yellowknife and Port Radium in the North West Territories wear G.W.G. ski slacks.

Miners and prospectors throughout the entire north country prefer the ski slack type of pants for winter wear.

Men and boys on the prairies are discovering that ski slacks are just the thing for outdoor work of all kinds as well as for school wear.

65-3-1—Men's navy blue melton ski slacks (for sports wear only) sizes 30 to 40 waist. Price, ... $5.00

66-3-1—Men's navy blue heavy weight northern ski slack for use where long wear is required. Sizes 30 to 40 waist. Price, ... $6.95

7-3-1—Boys' heavy navy blue frieze. Ages 6 to 10. Price, ... $3.75
Ages 11 to 16. Price, ... 4.95

16

"Bushmaster"
Suede Flannel Shirts

"Bushmaster" shirts are made from a medium weight tough suede cloth napped on both sides. They are of top grade workmanship and will give plenty of warmth and wear. Not shrunk. Available in the above attractive range of bright plain shades. Order by colour.

Men's, all colours. Sizes 14½ to 17½ Each.........................$1.50
Boys', Green, Royal, Tan, only. Sizes 6 to 10 years. Each.... 1.10
Youths', Green, Royal, Tan, only. Sizes 11 to 16 years. Each.. 1.25

Page 40

GWG Household Handbook,
1942, p. 40. RAM

TURNS STORMY TRIPS *AND* FROSTY CHORES *INTO* COSY TASKS

Zero days call for G.W.G. Parkas. They are standard equipment for cold weather outdoor work or driving.

Workers on Northern Canadian projects rely on the warmth and luxurious protection of Shearling-lined garments.

This Sheepskin-lined Parka Coat is 34 inches long. It has a heavy khaki shell of Sanforized drill. The body lining of warm curly sheepskin

comes well down over the hips. Has a buttoned front with leather loops. The parka hood has a drawstring and warm doeskin lining. The sleeves are doeskin lined. There are two large front pockets.

When the mercury settles down in the thermometer you'll be glad to have one of these G.W.G. Parkas.

Better prepare early. See your merchant about it soon.

THE GREAT WESTERN GARMENT CO., LTD., EDMONTON

THEY WEAR LONGER BECAUSE THEY'RE MADE STRONGER

Merchants who are now unable to buy stocks of G.W.G. goods, because of scarcity of supply or lack of established quota, should plan to acquire this brand for their stores when peace times return again.

Country Guide, November 1943. RAM

GWG Catalogue, 1950, p. 39. RAM

GWG Catalogue, 1950, p. 41. RAM

COWBOY UP!

From the mid-1940s through the 1970s, GWG ran a marketing campaign aimed at cowboys and rodeo fans. GWG received endorsements from rodeo champions and advertised its products through the Calgary Stampede, community rodeos, and later the Canadian Finals.

Various GWG ads of the 1940s and 1950s featured champion cowboys such as Bob Robinson, Frank Duce, Carl Olson, Red Kesler, Cody Morris, Gordon Earl, Wilf Gerlitz, and Doug Cosgrave's chuck wagon teams. Other advertisements were based on photographs of models, rather than real cowboys. The illustrations show a better fitting garment than the GWG's really were. Cowboys generally preferred the fit of Wrangler jeans, which had a lower rise and longer back curve than the GWGs.

GWG played a major role in supporting Western Canadian rodeos. The company distributed free rodeo program covers to local rodeos who added their name to the front and the program of events inside and supplied prizes and trophies at large events such as the Calgary Stampede. A 1953 Woodward's department store window display featured GWG western wear "donated…for all-round champion cowboy at the Edmonton rodeo." Jim Reinbold of Provost, Alberta, won the Saskatchewan Saddle Bronc Champion trophy saddle in Swift Current in 1967. During the 1970s, GWG sponsored the Canadian Finals Rodeo for three years. In 1975 GWG offered the major prizes for the championship events and claimed to be "Makers of the official CNFR jean."

GWG reached the larger country market through the radio. Early in his performing and songwriting career in the late 1940s, Stu Davis, Canada's Cowboy Troubadour, was known as GWG's Singing Cowboy. GWG sponsored a daily fifteen-minute program produced at CJCA Edmonton that aired in Regina, Calgary, and Edmonton. The 1948 *GWG Almanac* featured an image of Stu Davis and three pages of lyrics entitled, "The songs Stu Davis sings."

GWG also appealed to children who looked up to cowboys, initially through its sponsorship of the Lone Ranger radio program in the 1930s. A very popular role-playing game for young children for many years, "Cowboys and Indians" has now fallen out of fashion, but until the 1960s children dressed up in outfits and acted out their favourite Western characters. In Alberta, a boy's favourite Western character might well have been his father

or a local rodeo hero. Child-size leather chaps made by GWG were very good quality and might have been worn by young boys learning how to ride. GWG probably made the chaps to extend seasonal work in the leather department and to build brand loyalty among a young clientele. In the 1970s children could wear a belt buckle marked "Bunkhouse Bunch Member," a club sponsored by Woodward's, GWG, and the Canadian Finals Rodeo.

Champion Chuck Wagon Outfit, Calgary Stampede, *Country Guide*, June 1947. RAM

Country Guide, June 1948. RAM

Stu Davis, GWG Almanac,
1948. RAM

Advertising banner, 1950s. RAM, H08.17.215

Country Guide, June 1951. RAM

Woodward's window display, Edmonton, 1953.
Photograph by Alfred Blyth. PAA, BI2117

Country Guide, June 1956. RAM

Bob Robinson, 1956 Canadian Bronc Riding Championship.
Photograph by Alfred Blyth. PAA BI2360.1

143

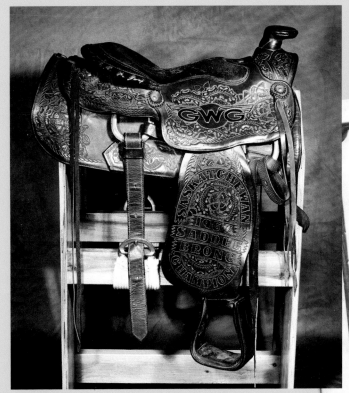

Saskatchewan Saddle Bronc Champion trophy
saddle presented by GWG, 1967. RAM, H08.17.247

Second Annual Canadian National Finals
Rodeo Program, 1975. RAM

THE CANADIAN NATIONAL FINALS
RODEO
FOR THE CHAMPIONSHIP OF CANADA

Canada's top cowboys compete
for the championship of Canada
in these nine championship events!

1. GWG SADDLE BRONC RIDING
2. GWG BAREBACK BRONC RIDING
3. GWG STEER WRESTLING
4. GWG CALF ROPING
5. GWG BULL RIDING
6. GWG NOVICE BRONC RIDING
7. GWG BOYS' STEER RIDING
8. GWG LADIES' BARREL RACING
9. GWG CUTTING HORSE

GWG

Makers of the official CNFR jean

PRINTED IN CANADA
metropolitan printing, edmonton, alberta

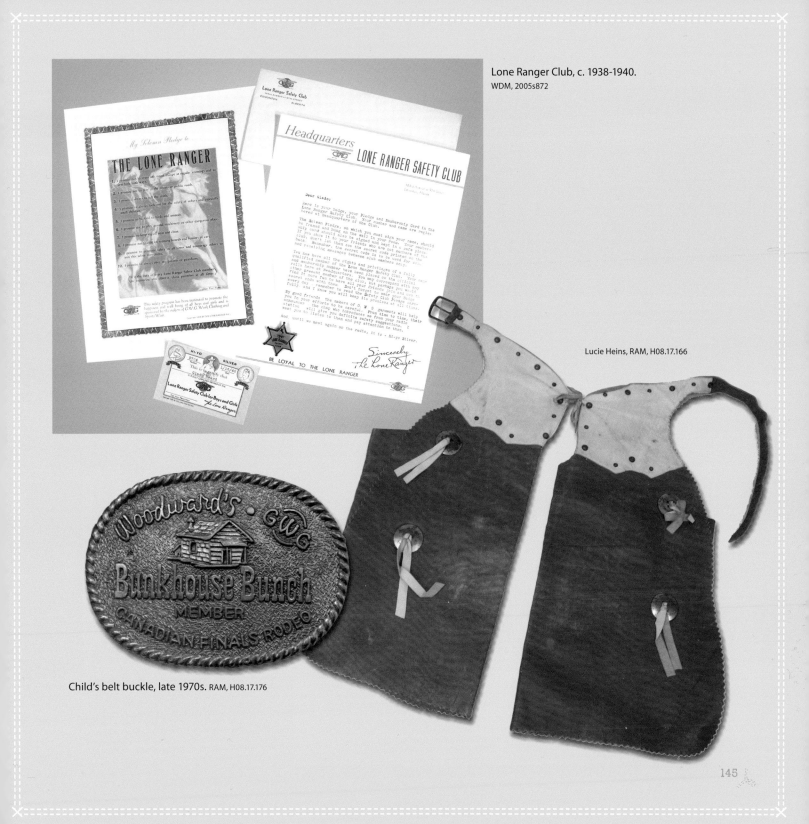

Lone Ranger Club, c. 1938-1940.
WDM, 2005s872

Lucie Heins, RAM, H08.17.166

Child's belt buckle, late 1970s. RAM, H08.17.176

145

MARKETING TO CANADIAN FAMILIES

Great Western Garment built its early reputation on high-quality men's and boys' workwear. During the Depression, in order to stay profitable, the company introduced new product lines, including women's and children's workwear and winter sportswear.

Although fabric for civilian clothing was rationed during World War II, GWG expanded its capacity to meet wartime demands for uniforms, and after the war, increased production of women's and children's casual clothing. GWG also broadened its marketing strategy in an effort to appeal to families throughout Canada rather than just to Western farmers, cowboys, and labourers.

Young women began wearing pants when working in factories during the war and continued to wear them for casual activities afterwards. Ladies wear was a branch of the clothing manufacturing industry distinct from workwear, but workwear companies were well equipped to produce women's sportswear. In the 1950s GWG introduced a number of brands for young women, such as Strapback and Frontier Queen, and emphasized that the fit and proportions were designed for women.

GWG shifted its advertising from regional agricultural publications to national media like *Maclean's*, the *Star Weekly*, and *National Home Monthly* as it extended distribution and sales throughout Canada. By 1961 GWG's casual clothing for the whole family was sold in fifty-five hundred retail outlets across Canada.

GWG Catalogue, 1938, p. 29. RAM

GWG Catalogue, 1939, p. 8. RAM

Farm Workshop Guide, 1946.
RAM

GWG Catalogue,
1950, p. 34. RAM

Star Weekly, 1950s. RAM

147

Star Weekly, 1950s. RAM

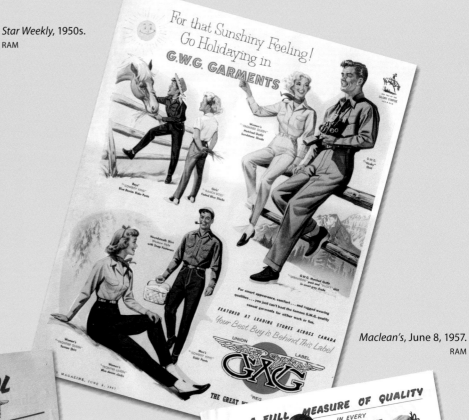

Maclean's, June 8, 1957. RAM

Star Weekly, August 18, 1956. RAM

Country Guide, September 1957. RAM

Country Guide, September 1957.
RAM

Maclean's,
August 15, 1959.
RAM

Maclean's,
June 6, 1959. RAM

Star Weekly, June 1, 1963.
RAM

149

CHAPTER FIVE

WHEN CLARENCE JACOX DIED in 1958, and J. Gerald Godsoe of Toronto succeeded him as president, the previously harmonious relationship between the workers and management deteriorated. Union minutes show that Godsoe did not get along as well with the union as had Jacox, and negotiations were sometimes difficult. During the 1960 negotiations, the union considered applying for conciliation. The most serious dispute between labour and management during this period ended in a work stoppage in the cutting room regarding piecework.

In 1962 a second round of acrimonious negotiations between Godsoe and the union's bargaining committee degenerated into personal attacks on union president Anne Baranyk. It was not simply a question of personalities. Godsoe expressed concern about both the future of GWG and the economic condition of Canada. The union countered that the company needed to support the workers, saying: "The previous threats of Hong Kong and Japan did not harm our business to any great extent."

Union secretary Louis Kabesh quoted Godsoe threatening that "Levi Strauss could send in their garments and close down the G.W.G. plant. They are now selling in Canada, but on a limited basis due to Mr. Godsoe's efforts." Godsoe demanded (and received) cooperation from the union, arguing that without it the company could not continue in business. Between the 1960 and 1962 negotiations, Levi's had quietly bought control of GWG.

Foreign Competition and Ownership

GWG's annual report notes that Levi Strauss & Co. bought 75 percent of GWG in 1961. C.A. Graham's widow and the Shaw family, her family, wanted to sell their shares. LS&CO. historian Lynn Downey notes that in the late 1950s, Levi Strauss & Co. started to look for opportunities to expand beyond the United States. The demand for Levi's internationally began with American soldiers wearing them during World War II and continued through the increasing dominance of American popular culture in the postwar period.

According to former GWG vice-president Don Freeland, Levi Strauss had investigated the idea of opening a plant in Calgary but realized that it could not compete with GWG, which had 85 percent of the Canadian jeans market. Levi Strauss benefited from the acquisition because it gave the company more access to the Canadian market. It allowed the company to more easily market its goods through Canadian stores, to compete with itself through GWG, and to undercut Canadian manufacturers. New owners Peter and Walter Haas joined the board, but GWG retained relatively independent management until the 1980s. Godsoe retained his position and shares in the company.

By 1961 GWG was one of Alberta's largest industrial enterprises, with 950 machine operators working day and night shifts. Production jumped from 8,000 units a day in 1958 to 13,000 five years later in 1963. GWG produced 20,000 units a day in 1968, compared to 25,000 units a week in 1940. This phenomenal escalation in production was due to time engineering and increased automation within the plant, as well as the increase in the number of operators.

To reflect an interest in expanding their market to all Canadians, in 1965 GWG changed the name of the popular Western brand Cowboy Kings to GWG Kings. Also that year, GWG updated its corporate identity, introducing a new streamlined logo with two straight lines, rather than wings, over the initials.

Many schools did not allow girls to wear pants because they were not feminine, or boys to wear blue jeans because of the rising association of blue jeans with rebellious youth. To counter restrictions against wearing blue jeans to school, GWG introduced coloured denim pants, and ran advertisements like the one that appeared in *Maclean's* August 15, 1959, pointing out that "they're worn everywhere...in the classroom...on the playing field...in your own back yard."

The union's concern about competition with imported goods continued to grow throughout the 1960s. In 1961 Local 120 proposed a resolution at the Alberta Federation of Labour convention dealing with protection from foreign imports for the clothing manufacturing trades. Unions tried to counter the threat from imported goods by encouraging Canadians to buy Canadian made, union made goods. However, the effectiveness of the union label in attracting sales even from other unionized workers declined through the 1950s to the extent that by the 1960s the union was reluctant to purchase the union made label from UGWA headquarters in New York.

Decline of the Union Made Label

Management supported the establishment of Local 120 UGWA in 1911 to enable GWG to use the union label. By the 1960s the label's influence had declined to a point where it no longer merited management support. In 1968 a UGWA display at the CTLC in Winnipeg continued unsuccessfully to encourage the use of the label. Local 120 Collection. PAA

GWG Replaces UGWA Label

The UGWA union made label was printed in the United States and shipped to Canadian locals to be sewn into union made garments. When Great Western Garment's market expanded beyond the working class, both the union and management were concerned that the labels were no longer worth the cost. GWG refused to pay for UGWA labels, but the union would not allow labels to be printed in Canada. GWG printed Union Made on its own labels rather than using a separate UGWA label. GWG Catalogue, 1960 back cover. RAM

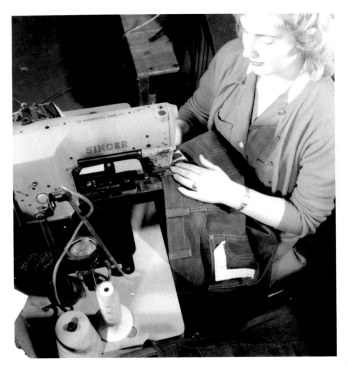

Speed-up, c. 1960-64

Time and motion studies were a feature of modern factories. By the 1960s GWG brought in engineers and introduced fully automated modern machines. The operators simply placed the fabric in the correct position. Operations were broken down into more and more steps throughout the company's transformation over the years, reducing the amount of time it took to manufacture a pair of jeans to seven and a half minutes when the plant closed. Levi's continued the trend begun by GWG.

LAC/National Film Board fonds/e002343821

Helen Krewenchuk

Long-term employee Helen Krewenchuk began working at GWG around 1948 and stayed until her retirement forty years later. She was quoted in *Common Threads*, Winter 1986, remembering that when she started, "They used to lock the doors, and even if you got to work half a minute past starting time, you'd have to go home or stay in the company cafeteria for half a day, with your pay docked accordingly. Once, I was late two days in a row because I slept in!"

Edmonton Journal, September 9, 1974. 07163FH

Asian Workers

RIGHT: Asian immigrants came from many countries including Hong Kong, China, Vietnam, Laos, and Cambodia. Few Asian workers participated in the union. Some did not attend meetings because they did not understand English. When the union translated meetings into Chinese they rarely attended because they were busy with young families, or working two jobs, or afraid to participate because of the political situations in the countries they had come from. Some underestimated the contribution of the union. Others with experience in non-unionized environments appreciated their work. *Edmonton Journal*, April 9, 1981. 07163G

BELOW: GWG promoted Asian workers to supervisory positions so they could communicate with the growing numbers of Asians working in the plant. Virginia Mah said that her wages dropped after becoming an instructor in 1973, so she went back to the line until the pay and benefits for instructors improved. By the 1980s the workforce at Edmonton's GWG was primarily Asian. Jean Mah, *Edmonton Journal*, April 9, 1981. 07163H

Increasingly Diverse Workforce

The history of immigration to Edmonton may be seen through the waves of garment workers who passed through the plant's doors. According to the municipal census, the city's population increased from 148,861 to 260, 733 in the 1950s largely due to immigration from Europe. Newcomers joined existing groups of employees. By the early 1960s, the workforce was comprised primarily of European immigrants and language became an important issue in the plant. However, Great Western Garment did little to accommodate newcomers until the late 1960s.

The first Chinese immigrants came to work at GWG in 1960, coinciding with GWG expanding its workforce and increasing production. For many, working at GWG was their first job in Canada. It was better than washing dishes; the work was hard but they were well paid and worked regular hours. For most of the twentieth century, Canada allowed immigration primarily from Europe. The federal government allowed a small number of Chinese people into Canada through family reunification provisions and arranged marriages after it repealed the Chinese Immigration Act in 1947. Hang Sau Mah, Chee Luck Mah, Sum Yuk Wong, and Mee Chan were among a handful of Chinese immigrants to work at GWG in the early 1960s.

In 1967 Canada adopted a merit-based point system for determining immigration with three categories of immigrants: Family, Refugee (later Humanitarian), and Independent, effectively eliminating institutionalized racism. For the first time, anyone who met the necessary qualifications could be considered for immigration. In the 1970s significant numbers of Chinese immigrants began moving to Edmonton. When Virginia Mah started working at GWG in 1970, there were fewer than twenty Chinese people working in the plant. She learned how to do several operations. Once large numbers of

Cowboys, 1965
To reflect their interest in expanding their market to all Canadians, in 1965 GWG changed the name of the popular Cowboy Kings to GWG Kings. However, the Western market remained important throughout the 1960s and 1970s. Hanna Kinsmen Round Up program, 1967. RAM

1964 Logo

Beginning in 1964, the logo changed several times. First, the feather wings became straight lines in an Art Deco style, over the initials GWG. As well as this company logo, individual GWG brands like Cowboy King and Iron Man featured their own distinct logos. GWG Catalogue, 1965, p. 4. RAM

1971 Logo

In 1971, in a further effort to modernize the brand, the wings were dropped altogether; the initials were more stylized and placed in front of a broken circle, rather than a solid dot. Lucie Heins, RAM, H08.17.117

Nev'R Press Pants

In 1965 GWG followed Levi Strauss's lead and was the first Canadian company to introduce permanent-press pants. Called Nev'R Press, the pants were treated through a high-temperature process that involved soaking garments in chemicals, then baking them. Unfortunately, the temperature was high for the workers as well. The area around the oven and presses that set the Nev'R Press pants was particularly hot. Temperatures rose to over 32° Celsius. After a few years, they moved the machines to a separate finishing plant and the union negotiated extra breaks for those working on Nev'R Press pants. The Compensation Board looked into the heat problem at the request of the union. By 1970 50 percent of garments were made of Koratron, a wrinkle- and soil-resistant fabric. GWG Catalogue, 1965. RAM

Chinese applicants began to work there in the late 1970s, Mah became an instructor. She translated during job interviews and trained the new workers.

She said that she liked both roles: "I liked to be sewing machine operator because I just sit down and do my job, try to do the best I can, the fastest I can. I don't have to worry about anything, don't have to socialize with anybody. As an instructor, I liked too, because you have your own trainees you can go and take care of them to help them out, to train them. You have a whole bunch of instructors and supervisors during break time to socialize. It's different. I liked both."

Sum Yuk Wong compared the importance of caring about your work in the factory with caring for a chicken, noting, "If the chicken dies, then how can you have eggs to eat?"

The women would sit together in the cafeteria at lunchtime with others who spoke the same language. Hana Razga, who came to Edmonton from Prague in 1968 following the Czechoslovakian revolution, said, "I felt it was like a Babylon...number of languages." The immigrants worked very hard to ensure education and career opportunities for their children, many of whom have prospered in Canada.

As each immigrant group came to Edmonton, family, community members, government, and later, immigrant services agencies advised newcomers to apply for work at GWG. GWG began hiring through the National Employment Service, which Razga noted sent non-English-speaking immigrant women to GWG for employment regardless of how well educated they were.

Chinese immigrants and Asian refugees from Vietnam, Laos, and Cambodia, who began coming to Edmonton in the late 1970s, often worked two jobs to send money home to support their families or to save enough money to sponsor their families to come to Canada. Many of them found working in a largely female environment, with women who

had similar challenges and concerns for families far away, comforting. Immigrant workers were content to work in a unionized plant. They earned decent wages and worked in a safe environment with on-site health care rather than in a sweatshop.

There was a lot of turnover at the plant. Not everyone could adjust to the work or the working environment. Hiring, training, and retaining enough workers always posed a challenge. While some workers were loyal to the company and stayed there for years, others quit after just a few weeks, often at the end of their training period when they had to switch from hourly wages to piecework and were unable to work fast enough to earn a decent living. Some left at their first lunch hour and never returned.

The Great Western Garment factory reached capacity and the company considered expanding the plant. Great Western Garment had approximately twelve hundred workers, with machine operators working day or night shifts. Nurse Yeandle arranged for trainers from St. John Ambulance to come in and provide first aid training to supervisors on the night shift because she did not work at night.

Janet Cardinal recalled that when she started working as an operator at the plant in 1962, she was overwhelmed by the size of the factory. "I'll never forget the first day I started there. It was so big and massive and they took me way down to the far end to where I was going to be sewing and they showed me on my way there where the washroom was, but I was too afraid to leave my machine to go the washroom because I knew I'd never find my way back again."

Newspaper accounts note that the company wanted to hire at least two hundred more workers but immigration had fallen off in the late fifties and early sixties. As well, immigration policies precluded the plant from importing skilled needle trade workers. The federal government did not

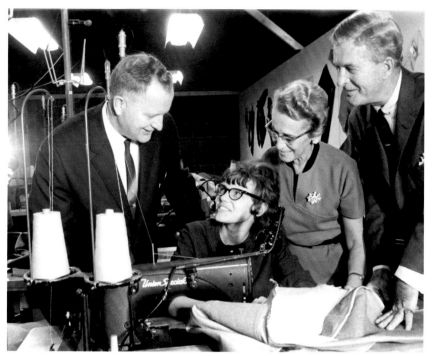

Vocational Training, 1965
In 1965 GWG became the first company to partner with the provincial government to train unemployed and underemployed people. Trainees were paid minimum wage, half of which was paid by the provincial government, and that was reimbursed by the federal government under the vocational education agreements. LEFT TO RIGHT: Minister of Education R.H. McKinnon, machine operator Mrs. R. Taylor, Supervisor Mrs. E.C. Nufer, and GWG President J.G. Godsoe. *Edmonton Journal.* PAA 071631

encourage immigrants to settle in Alberta, where the economy was primarily agricultural and resource-based. Great Western Garment lobbied the government unsuccessfully to relax its regulations and allow more female immigrant factory workers to settle in Alberta.

In 1963 GWG began discussions with the Northern Alberta Institute of Technology (NAIT) and the provincial government to address the lack of trained labour in Alberta. Great Western Garment set up the first cost-sharing agreement between the provincial government and industry. The provincial government paid half of the minimum wage of trainees and instructors—the federal government reimbursed the province under vocational education agreements. GWG taught women the sewing trade in a three-month training program. GWG paid trainees less than minimum wage. Anne Ozipko noted that she earned forty-five cents an hour, fifteen

cents below minimum wage. She had worked at GWG for three and a half years in the 1940s and was not really in training. The Edmonton and District Labour Council and the union lobbied the Labour Board to rescind the agreement, but it took several years.

In 1965 a basic English course for new Canadians was added to the vocational training program and was later extended to all company manufacturing facilities. Women who had just arrived in Canada and did not speak English received thirty-six hours of language training. In April 1967 the federal Canada Manpower Centre assumed responsibility for the joint operation of the training centre from the provincial Department of Education. The federal and provincial governments and GWG jointly financed the program.

The continuing labour shortage in Edmonton and Alberta delayed planned expansion of the plant. After considering establishing branch plants in several Alberta communities, including Wetaskiwin, Camrose, and Red Deer, GWG purchased a manufacturing company in Brantford, and first contracted out, then purchased, another company in Winnipeg. There were not enough potential workers in any of the Alberta cities to operate a branch plant in Alberta, so GWG decided instead to expand in Central Canada.

Kitchen-Peabody

The *Edmonton Journal* noted that in August 1965 GWG acquired the Kitchen-Peabody factory in Brantford, Ontario. The acquisition followed a failed effort by a group of Kitchen-Peabody and GWG employees to purchase the company. When Godsoe learned of their intentions, he alerted Levi Strauss & Co., which immediately provided the funding necessary for GWG to purchase the company.

Kitchen-Peabody had been founded in 1911 as the Kitchen Overall and Shirt Co. on Dalhousie Street. Kitchen relocated to the Cockshutt Building at 11 Queen Street, and in 1917 moved into the 2,040-square metre former Buck foundry building on West Street. It was known for its Railroad Signal overalls and workmen's shirts. In 1924 Kitchen acquired Peabody's Ltd. The company remained in the family until Howard D. Daniels and A. Bradshaw and Sons Ltd. of Toronto bought it in 1946. In 1949 the Amalgamated Clothing Workers of America (ACWA) organized the plant as Local 551. In September 1955 Kitchen moved to a 6,690-square metre factory at 5 Edward Street, and in September 1962 the company changed its name to Kitchen-Peabody Garments Limited to reflect the fact that overalls no longer represented a significant portion of their business.

After GWG purchased the plant, it initially continued to operate under the Kitchen-Peabody name and retained its own management. Great Western Garment centralized the production of work garments in this plant, employing three hundred women, rearranged the assembly lines in the shirt and pants departments, and retrained workers to increase production by adopting the highly engineered manufacturing process used by GWG.

Kitchen-Peabody became the Great Western Garment Co. [Brantford] in 1968. Mike May, who had been with the Ontario company for many years, became general manager. Within a few years, the plant not only produced men's work clothing, but women's and children's casual clothing, and the workforce increased to 350 people.

Winnipeg Pants

Edmonton's labour shortage continued. Winnipeg had become Canada's leading producer of menswear in the mid-1950s. Therefore, in 1965, GWG began contracting production from Winnipeg Pants Manufacturing Company, as noted in union minutes. The firm was founded in 1939 by Abraham Rich and his brother-in-law Ben Kettner and located on the seventh floor of the Whitla Building at 70 Arthur Street, in the heart of the warehouse district. The Companies Office in Manitoba notes that Great Western Garment (Winnipeg) Limited was incorporated on March 2, 1967.

David Rich remembered that GWG purchased the pants side of Winnipeg Pants from his father Abraham Rich, who stayed on for a few years as vice-president and general manager. In addition to Rich, the other four original directors were from Edmonton: President J. Gerald Godsoe, Russell Gormley, Roger Roscoe, and W.B. Shaw. Great Western Garment (Winnipeg) Limited moved to larger facilities on the fourth and fifth floors of the Apparel Mart Building at 85 Adelaide Street on the northeast corner of McDermot

Avenue, a centre for garment industry manufacturers and importers. David Rich retained the jacket manufacturing portion of the business, which is still operated in the same building under the name Richlu Manufacturing.

Foreign Competition

Great Western Garment continued to lobby the federal government to revise immigration requirements. The *Edmonton Journal*, January 24, 1967, noted the company's argument that the federal government's new immigration policies "preclude the 'import' of skilled needle trade workers.... GWG expects some government aid to overcome the manpower problem.... The federal government will be asked to lower immigration entrance requirements — currently grade 11 — to boost emigration from Europe, Central America and Asia, the industries' traditional labor pool."

Ironically, the demand to lower immigration requirements was fuelled by competition from foreign imports. GWG wanted to import the workers themselves, not the manufactured goods. Many of the countries from which they originated did not provide comparable benefits and were therefore able to sell goods at a much lower cost. However, GWG could not keep up with demand locally and contracted work out.

GWG used to make the best overalls, Ozipko remembered. "Then they contracted them out to China.... When they came back from China, the straps were too short, the legs were too narrow.... So the carpenters stopped buying them." On another occasion, they contracted out an order of green work pants to China. "When it came back, they were ashamed to put their label on them because they had so many things

GWG Acquired Kitchen-Peabody, Brantford, Ontario, 1965
Like GWG, the Kitchen Overall and Shirt Co. was established in 1911. In 1924 Kitchen acquired Peabody's and the company became Kitchen-Peabody. Howard D. Daniels and A. Bradshaw and Sons Ltd. of Toronto purchased the company and Daniels became general manager. When GWG acquired Kitchen-Peabody, Daniels stayed on at the Edward Street plant until 1968, when Mike May became general manager. Workers at the Brantford plant respected Daniels.
Courtesy of Daniels Family

Great Western Garment (Manitoba) Ltd.
GWG purchased Winnipeg Pants from Abraham Rich in
1967. The company moved to larger facilities in the Apparel
Mart Building at the corner of Adelaide Street and McDermot
Avenue, and in 1977 moved to this factory at 365 Bannatyne
Avenue, the former Stovel Company Building shown shortly
after its construction in 1916. By then GWG was the largest
garment manufacturing plant in Winnipeg with over three
hundred workers, unionized under the Amalgamated
Clothing Workers of America. Murray Peterson Collection

wrong with them. They gave the whole shebang to the Work
Warehouse and told them to sell them as seconds."

An article in the *Edmonton Journal*, May 16, 1967, underlined GWG's concerns about competition. It noted that
GWG laid off workers at the Brantford plant and reduced
the workforce at the Edmonton plant from thirteen hundred
to eleven hundred employees in the past year. Vice-President
Gormley was quoted saying, "It all depends how much we feel
the hot breath of imports. A shipload of Asian textiles may
have arrived in Vancouver this morning and one of our large
department store customers may fail to renew an order."

In 1968 GWG improved production and distribution
efficiency in order to compete with imports particularly
from Japan, Hong Kong, and China. GWG opened a $1
million, two-storey, 9,850-square metre warehouse in
the Strathcona Industrial Park in Edmonton at 4040-98
Street, with funding from the Department of Industry and
Development. Marathon Realty owned the building which
was custom-built and leased to GWG.

GWG consolidated the storage and distribution of
GWG garments produced at the Brantford, Winnipeg, and
Edmonton plants and had seventeen regional sales offices
across the country. GWG transformed sales to retail stores.
In the 1960s Floyd Nattrass of GWG developed the Safety
Stock Analysis Forecast and Earnings System (SAFE) whereby
salesmen kept track of what various stores ordered. They
would go into the stores, count the inventory, and tell the
merchants how many of which styles and sizes to order.
GWG salesmen travelled the back roads visiting towns so
small that former salesman Dale Pearn recounted they used
to say, "only the guys from GWG, Stanfield's [underwear],
and God know where these places are."

GWG acquired a UNIVAC 9400, the most advanced
computer system available, and had its own fleet of trucks

Expansion in Edmonton, 1968

In 1968 GWG opened a $1 million, two-storey, 9,850-square metre warehouse in Edmonton. The provincial government provided funding towards construction through the Department of Industry and Development, which was at the time encouraging the growth of secondary industries in the province. In 1973 GWG established a $500,000 cutting centre in the same part of the city and removed the cutters from the plant to allow room for another production line. *Edmonton Journal.* PAA, J181.1

Distribution Centre, 1968

GWG consolidated the storage and distribution of garments produced at the Brantford, Winnipeg, and Edmonton plants in the Edmonton distribution centre. *Edmonton Journal.* PAA, J181.5

GWG Trucks, 1968

GWG acquired its own fleet of trucks to transport goods between Edmonton and the Brantford and Winnipeg plants. Jean Binette started work in the distribution centre in 1977 managing the trucking division, and eventually became the plant manager. *Edmonton Journal.* 07163E

transporting garments between plants. Newspaper accounts of the opening noted that the provincial government supported the project in an effort to diversify Alberta's economy by encouraging the growth of secondary industries in the province.

The *Edmonton Journal*, March 14, 1968, noted that Great Western Garment was the largest employer of women in Western Canada. By 1970 the plant employed immigrants from nearly twenty countries. In order to attract and retain workers, GWG looked into providing on-site daycare in the plant.

The Youth Market

One of the new brands introduced in the late 1960s was the Peace Jean. The Peace Jean was a low-rise jean, slim leg with a flair at the hem, and a button closure—no fly over the buttons. They came out first in denim, then in different colours and patterns. They took off.

The GWG account was the second largest marketing account in Alberta next to the provincial government. After more than thirty years with the same firm, Vice-President Merchandising Don Freeland decided that it was time for a change in order to attract the youth market. GWG moved its lucrative marketing contract to Goodis, Goldberg, Soren Ltd.

In 1972 Freeland and his wife went to Europe to get some fresh ideas. They were walking down the street in Venice one day when he noticed a store selling used jeans at high prices. He thought about the fact that his wife always pre-washed jeans before their children wore them. New denim was stiff and scratchy because the warp threads were soaked in potato starch to prevent them from breaking when the fabric was woven. Freeland returned to Edmonton and experimented with pre-washing jeans. The first cleaner he called refused when asked to wash 160,000 pairs! Eventually Freeland found

someone willing to try, and after trial and error, achieved a nice soft effect.

Freeland tested out several names on a group of young people who loved the concept, but not the names: Wash Out, Bleach Out, and Softies. Someone suggested Scrubs, and then Scrubbies. He introduced them in a few stores in Toronto, and then Eaton's Montreal store ordered nine hundred pairs. According to Freeland, "It was unpacked on Friday. It hit the shelves. By Saturday, there wasn't one pair left. Never happened before in their history. French kids will die for fashion....We were washing sixteen thousand pairs a day when I left the company."

GWG ran the first national television campaign for jeans and introduced four radio advertisements for Scrubbies. In this case, GWG was ahead of Levi Strauss. Other jean companies, such as Faded Glory and Britannia jeans, immediately knocked off the concept, but Freeland said Levi Strauss initially thought pre-washed jeans were just a fad and was reluctant to follow suit. As part of its efforts to modernize the company brand, GWG formally dropped the words Great, Western, and Garment. The Brantford plant changed its name to GWG Eastern Limited in 1970. The Edmonton and Winnipeg plants changed to GWG Limited in 1971. In Brantford as in Edmonton and Winnipeg, GWG introduced automated machinery as soon as it became available. Automated machines included cloth spreaders, pocket setters, and machines with automatic positioners and trimmers.

Although there were many long-term employees, staff turnover was high. Brenda Bridgewater, who was a supervisor in Brantford at the time, remembered from training new employees that, "if they didn't come back from break, you weren't surprised." The company tried to accommodate workers and their families, for example,

Peace Jeans: "Hell No, We Won't Go," c. 1970
In 1965 the Americans began fighting in Vietnam. The peace movement mobilized around marches and protests in both the United States and Canada. Demonstrators sang Country Joe McDonald's, "And it's one, two, three, what are we fightin' for? Don't ask me I don't give a damn! Next stop is Vietnam!" The "upside down Y" peace symbol became ubiquitous as a fashion statement. To appeal to a young, politically conscious market, GWG introduced a low-rise fashion jean called Peace Jeans that featured the peace symbol on the fly buttons and proved to be a very hot seller.
Lucie Heins, RAM, H08.17.59

allowing one operator to work alone at night serging slash pockets, but with operators working on an assembly line, the jobs lacked flexibility.

Bought Out by Levi Strauss

In this era, the biggest impact of foreign competition was from the United States, not Asia. In 1972 Levi's bought the remaining 25 percent of GWG Limited for $2.75 million and GWG Limited became a wholly owned subsidiary. This acquisition was a part of Levi's expansion during the 1970s that, according to *Menswear Magazine*, saw annual sales rise from $432 million in 1971 to $2.85 billion in 1981. Newspaper accounts note that GWG retained its Canadian directorship. Russell Gormley, who had been vice-president since 1966, became president of GWG Limited, and the head

office remained in Edmonton. GWG continued to operate independently of Levi's.

Levi Strauss & Co. (Canada) Inc. incorporated, and with funding from the federal Department of Regional Economic Expansion built a 4,180-square metre warehouse and plant in Cornwall, Ontario, to manufacture Levi's jeans. Initially, the Cornwall plant provided a means for Levi's to import products manufactured in plants outside North America.

The federal government protected Canada's textile and garment industries through quotas on imported clothing until the introduction of the Canada-US Free Trade Agreement (FTA) in 1987 and the North American Free Trade Agreement (NAFTA) in 1993. By establishing the plant, Levi's was able to import goods into Canada and compete directly against now Levi-owned GWG Limited. Initially Levi's derived 96 percent of sales from imported goods, and only 4 percent from goods

Here are the styles that sent GWG's swinging musical jingle to the top of the Hit Parade!

GEORGE W. GROOVEY FLARES—"THE FIT THAT JUST WON'T QUIT!" Youth-oriented, up-tempo slacks and jeans that "turn on" young hearts who are looking for the latest in fashion and fabric. These are a few of the favorites: new styles are available every month. Pinto Denims, Tie-Dyes, Bleach-outs, Bold Stripes—you name it, your GWG dealer has a wide choice.

18. **WIDE TRACKS**—basketweave Cotton and Nylon fabric that's sturdy and stylish. White ground with wide coloured stripes in Blue, Brown, Green, Gold or Maroon.
SIZES 28 to 36 .... 12.95

19. **NEV'R-PRESS CANVAS** — Fortrel/Cotton with a one-year guarantee of performance. Blue, Brown, Green, Gold or White.
SIZES 28 to 36 .... 10.95

PINTO DENIM—GWG's exclusive bleached, sueded Blue Cotton denim that's sweeping the country in popularity!

20. Boys' sizes 7-12 .... 7.95
    Youths' sizes 13-16 .... 8.95

21. Men's sizes 28-36 .... 10.95

GEORGE W. GROOVEY FLARES—"LES PANTALONS A JAMAIS ELEGANTS!" **Des styles GWG en tête de la Parade des Succès!** Pantalons et jeans au rythme du temps, séduisant les jeunes coeurs à la recherche de modes et tissus nouveaux. Voici quelques-uns des nouveaux styles, les favoris disponibles chaque mois. Pinto Denims, Tie-Dyes, Bleach-outs, Bold Stripes, tout ce que vous désirez—votre concessionaire GWG possède le choix.

18. **WIDE TRACKS**—Tissu "basketweave" de coton et nylon solide et élégant! Fond blanc à larges lignes bleu, brun, vert, or ou marron.
TAILLES 28 à 36 .... 12.95

19. **NEV'R-PRESS CANVAS**—Fortrel/Coton, portant un an de garantie de rendement. Bleu, brun, vert, or ou blanc.
TAILLES 28 à 36 .... 10.95

PINTO DENIM—Le denim en suédine de coton bleu; décoloration exclusive GWG, balayant le pays de sa popularité.

20. Tailles garçonnets 7-12 .... 7.95
    Jeunes gens—tailles 13-16 .... 8.95

21. Tailles pour hommes 28-36 .... 10.95

George W. Groovey, 1970
Having dropped the words Great Western Garment from its company name, GWG introduced George W. Groovey and the less known Grace W. Groovey in 1970. GWG attempted to get away from the now old and conservative sounding Great Western Garment and appeal to a younger market. A street busker in Greenwich Village, New York City, wrote the soon very popular, award-winning radio jingle, "You can be George W. Groovey in your GWGs." GWG Catalogue, 1970, p. 6. RAM

Anything Goes, 1971
In August 1971 GWG ran an ad in the program for an Edmonton Eskimos vs. Calgary Stampeders' football game that said, "Anything Goes," and featured a topless woman shown from the back, in wild floral pants. The text read: "When we say anything goes, we mean GWG's go with anything. Or anyone." This very racy ad was oriented towards a young, male market. It was a complete departure from staid overalls and work pants ads that first built GWG loyalty among their fathers' generation. Edmonton Eskimos vs. Calgary Stampeders program, Vol. 2. No. 4, August 11, 1971, p. 17. RAM

Scrubbies, 1972

The original pre-washed jeans were invented by then Vice-President of Merchandising Don Freeland. Scrubbies became GWG's most popular brand and began a revolution in the treatment of fashion jeans. Here, Don Freeland poses with a pair of Scrubbies from an article in the *Edmonton Journal*, January 27, 1977.

Courtesy of Don Freeland

manufactured in Cornwall, but soon the plant was operating at full capacity.

With 375 workers at the Edward Street plant, GWG constructed a 2,560-square metre plant on Elgin Road in Brantford and purchased an adjacent single hectare to allow for future expansion. When the plant opened in January 1973 with 150 workers, a zipper opening fittingly replaced the traditional ribbon cutting ceremony. It was the first plant in Brantford to be air-conditioned. Initially, Edward Street manufactured casual wear and Elgin Street manufactured jeans.

By retaining the GWG name in Brantford and Edmonton and independent management, Levi's was able to access Canadian government funds. The provincial government provided a $100,000 Ontario Development Corporation grant. Articles in the *Globe and Mail* and *Brantford Expositor* note that local manufacturers accused the government of undercutting Canadian manufacturers through their support of an American-owned company. The government claimed it was unaware that Levi Strauss owned GWG.

In 1973 GWG built a $500,000 cutting plant at 4104-99 Street in Edmonton's Strathcona Industrial Park. This allowed the company to remove the cutting function from the main plant and dedicate more space to sewing machinery.

In January 1973 GWG leased a temporary factory in an existing building on Duchess Street in Saskatoon, and began hiring and training operators — one hundred workers over the next ten months — while building a new facility on a hectare of property at the corner of 34 Street and Ontario Avenue. The city encouraged GWG to locate in Saskatoon by acquiring the land and turning it over at cost. GWG received a $229,000 Department of Regional Economic Expansion (DREE) grant for its construction. Edmonton-based Bentall Engineering drafted the plans and supervised construction of

Saskatoon Plant, 1973

GWG opened a 16,764-square metre, $1.25 million plant in Saskatoon in November 1973. There were 350 operators on staff. The company's optimistic plan to double the size of the plant and employ up to 480 people never materialized. Instead, the factory closed in July 1982. The workforce in Saskatoon, like Edmonton, was predominantly immigrant women. Recent immigrants comprised less than 8 percent of the city's population but 67 percent of the plant's workforce.

Saskatoon Public Library-Local History Room, cp-6747-3-b

the 16,764-square metre, $1.25 million building that opened November 30, 1973.

The Saskatoon plant produced 3,500 pairs of blue jeans per day and 70,000 pairs per month. The workforce was expected to grow from 120 to 250 workers fairly quickly. The plant employed both Canadians and recent immigrants, with Vietnamese and Filipinos being the two most prevalent groups. The United Garment Workers of America organized the Saskatoon plant as Local 486. Levi Strauss & Co. (Canada) Inc. leased a factory in Stoney Creek, Ontario, in 1975.

Like Edmonton, the Brantford plants advertised in several languages and hired many immigrant workers. They overcame the language barrier by using training films to show workers how to operate machinery. Work was steady. Whether due to denim shortages or to reduce inventory, GWG occasionally laid workers off during the 1970s. Labour relations in the Brantford plant were also stable, with only one dispute recorded. The Brantford Local 551 of the Amalgamated Clothing Workers of America had a one-day strike in 1975 over an illegal vote to ratify their contract. As a result, management and the union reopened negotiations.

By 1974 GWG had become the largest garment manu-facturing plant in Winnipeg with over three hundred workers, up from approximately eighty when GWG acquired Winnipeg Pants. Like the GWG workers in Brantford, they were unionized under the Amalgamated Clothing Workers of America. In 1977 the company purchased a large factory, constructed of brick and concrete, which had originally housed a printing firm. GWG moved its operations, including its sales office, to its new address at 365 Bannatyne Avenue. The company continued to operate out of this location until the early 1980s, when GWG decided to close the plant because of what local manager Ken Jones called an "outdated" plant that the company could not expand. Despite the efforts of civic and provincial governments, GWG closed its doors on January 10, 1984, putting 245 workers out of jobs. In addition to the GWG plants, the company contracted production to a number of manufacturers in Canada. For example, Lindsay, Ontario manufactured the Western style shirts, and London, Ontario manufactured coveralls. The GWG work represented between 75 percent and 100 percent of their production. Locally, GWG contracted finishing out to Western Linen.

Articles in the *Globe and Mail* and *Edmonton Journal* detailed Levi's and GWG's legal difficulties. Levi's was convicted at least twice under the Combines Investigation Act in the 1970s. Levi's also faced charges of price fixing in 1974. In 1977 GWG Ltd. was fined $21,000 after pleading guilty to two charges of price fixing, and in 1979 Levi Strauss & Co. (Canada) Inc. was fined $150,000 — the largest fine ever imposed in Canada for price maintenance.

Consolidation

GWG Limited and GWG (Eastern) Limited amalgamated on December 1, 1978, under the name GWG Limited with Erwin Mertens as president. Anne Ozipko noted that around 1980 GWG introduced a benefit package that included paid sick leave and long-term disability. The company and the workers each paid half of the health care benefit. In the late 1980s it was the first garment manufacturing company in North America to get a dental plan. The company paid 80 percent and employees paid 20 percent. They adjusted the workers' hours so they worked from 7:00 a.m. to 4:00 p.m., with a half-hour lunch break, and finished work at 1:00 p.m. on Fridays, which gave them a half day for various appointments.

In Brantford, the number of workers increased from 137 in 1975 to approximately 500 in 1979. GWG became well respected in Brantford and Edmonton for its community service. One of the most visible features introduced by Levi Strauss to its Canadian subsidiaries was the Community Involvement Teams (CIT). Originated in California in 1970, beginning in the late 1970s CITs provided a structure for workers to raise funds for numerous causes, both locally and internationally, with the support of the company. The Human Resources manager and workers in the plant established the funding priorities. In later years, they supported the Mennonite Centre for Newcomers, battered women's shelters, and inner-city lunch programs. Working with the Muttart Foundation, they started the Kids in the Hall restaurant in City Hall, training inner-city youth to work in a restaurant. Levi's did not use the program as a promotional vehicle. The employees rather than the company presented the cheques.

Levi Strauss Canada Inc. took over management of the Brantford plants from GWG in January 1980. GWG opened a second plant in Brantford on Elgin Street. Peter Haas of Levi Strauss in San Francisco pushed expansion of the Elgin Street plant after seeing the working conditions at Edward Street. He wanted to close the old plant on Edward Street and consolidate manufacturing in one location.

The Edward Street plant switched from producing shirts, jackets, and work pants to jeans as an interim step prior to closing the plant. In May 1981 they opened a $2.2 million, 9,760-square metre facility — four times the size of the original plant — which employed three hundred workers. GWG reduced the time required to manufacture a pair of jeans to twelve minutes. However, the operation was short-lived.

Workers had had difficulty establishing fair prices and adapting to new machinery after the company changed its production from casual to fashionable clothing, and went on

ANNE OZIPKO

Anne Ozipko came to Canada as a child in 1930 from the Ukraine. She grew up in the Boyle area and came to Edmonton after leaving school. She worked at GWG from May 1943 until she had her first child in February 1947. Her first job was topstitching inseams. Her next job was sewing the inseams. In 1963 Ozipko returned to GWG to supplement her husband's income, put her son through university, and buy a piano for her daughters. She stayed forty years until she retired in 1997.

Ozipko worked on the night shift and soon became shop steward. She became a utility girl, someone who could operate every machine in the plant. GWG asked Ozipko three times to be a supervisor, but she was offered less money than she was making on piecework so she declined.

She became president of the union in 1970, and began working full-time for the union in 1978. She became the union representative on the Unemployment Insurance Board of Referees in 1986, a position she held for twenty years. In 1987 she became the Canadian representative to UGWA headquarters in New York. Ozipko was most proud of her role in changing from the piecework system. She acknowledged that the quota system was not perfect, but "people didn't have to work like dogs to get what they wanted to get."

UFCW Local 120G full-time representative Anne Ozipko (left) with Levi Strauss worker Ana Silva, who printed care labels for the Levi Strauss products.
UFCW Canada Action, United Food and Commercial Workers, Canada

an illegal strike. Within the year, the plant closed and GWG laid off 268 employees as a result of consolidating production of different lines in specific plants. In 1981 Levis Strauss Canada Inc. opened a new finishing centre at 70 Easton Road, a $2.1 million project. Levi's contracted out production of shirts, T-shirts, hats, and some bottoms to a number of different companies. In 1981 Levi's was quoted in the *Globe and Mail*, saying that its policy was "as much as possible, manufacture locally for the local market and buy textiles locally.... (One exception is shirts and tops, because making them 'is far more competitive, volatile and changing' and they do not provide the same return on capital investment)." However, Larry Gobeil, manager of the Winnipeg plant from 1971 to 1978, remembers being criticized by senior management for stating in a media interview that the plant purchased its denim from Mexico. At the time, GWG purchased the entire inventory of the Mexican plant.

Great Northern Apparel

In 1982, due to the economic recession at the time, Levi's established Great Northern Apparel Inc. (GNA) with its head office in Toronto as a holding company for GWG Inc. and Levi Strauss & Co. (Canada) Inc. to reduce duplication between the two companies. The establishment of a separate company, rather than simply absorbing GWG within Levi's, smoothed the transition for workers who were very loyal to one or the other company.

Although Levi's had said that the two companies would continue to operate autonomous marketing divisions, the *Edmonton Journal* noted on September 27, 1982, that GWG had laid off fifty employees as the

GWG **Jeans**
Fit where it counts

GWG LIMITED — 5240 - CALGARY TRAIL
EDMONTON

* "GWG JEANS" IS A REGISTERED TRADEMARK OF GWG LTD

Femme Fit, 1980

GWG went to great lengths to reach beyond the work clothes and Western wear markets. In 1980 GWG introduced Femme Fit jeans, designed to fit a woman's body. This avant-garde advertisement appeared in a ladies' magazine, possibly *Chatelaine*. This is the first GWG ad located that features a black model. The 1980 GWG Catalogue also featured an Asian model.

Private Collection

INTRODUCING GWG **FEMME FIT**
Jeans made to fit women.
A narrower waist for a neater look.
Ask for them at your favorite jeans store.

Bum Bums, 1980

In 1980 GWG introduced Bum Bums, a brand that gained some notoriety through a controversial television commercial in which a number of different models walked away from the camera—all, of course, wearing Bum Bums. Some felt the ad debased the British patriotic song "Land of Hope and Glory." GWG also initiated a Bum Bums competition as part of the Canadian Finals Rodeo, where people lined up across the stage and the audience compared bums. This print ad was in use before the Bum Bums brand name, but is in a similar vein to the television commercial. Canadian Finals Rodeo program, 1979. RAM company began to transfer management, marketing, and sales functions to the new headquarters in Toronto. The majority of GNA management were former GWG workers. A number of other senior employees in Edmonton were offered positions in Toronto but chose not to relocate.

Former GWG vice-president merchandising Don Freeland and salesman Dale Pearn felt that Levi's deliberately played down the GWG brand to focus on Levi's. Freeland said that GWG's sales dropped from $81 million to $0.5 in a year and a half as a result. Rodeo champion and salesman at different times for Levi's, Wrangler, and GWG, Bob Robinson noted that Levi's paid salesmen a salary and capped their earnings. GWG had paid salesmen commission, allowing them to earn a lot of money, something Freeland had argued about with Levi's.

They closed the Saskatoon plant in July 1982 and the Winnipeg plant in January 1984. Reports circulated in Edmonton concerning possible closure in 1983. The *Edmonton Journal* quoted GWG Inc.'s President Erwin Mertens, May 13, 1982, saying that, "The proportion of imports to domestically produced apparel is constantly increasing. At some point in the last three years, the domestic goods were over 60 per cent of the total market. Now it is estimated in the mid-50s."

Jean Binette became manager of the Edmonton plant in 1982, and from the beginning, had a good relationship with the union. Binette noted that the union and management had the same goals. "We wanted to make sure the employees were treated fairly, we wanted to make sure that the plant was successful, and that we were able to produce, to be flexible in our production, and produce anything that was required at a good cost, and with good quality." GWG had always been very conscious of its competition, whether from Winnipeg, the United States, or the developing world. The 1980s began a challenging period that required collaboration between the union and management.

Binette and union leader Anne Ozipko met weekly to resolve any issues that Human Resources could not handle. From then on there were no written grievances in the plant. Management kept no secrets from the union. Ozipko said that he was the first manager who acknowledged how hard the operators worked and appreciated it.

In 1983 the Canadian Division was only 3.5 percent of the overall Levi Strauss business — significantly smaller than operations in the United States (Jeanswear 37.1 percent, Menswear 8 percent, Womenswear 10.6 percent, and Youthwear 11.5 percent) and Europe (15.2 percent), comparable with the Asia/Pacific (3.5 percent) and Latin America (3.4 percent) Divisions. Levi Strauss and Co.'s Annual Report indicates that the Levis Strauss USA sales were more than $1.8 billion compared to approximately $400 million for the European Operations, and $100 million each for Canada, Asia/Pacific, and Latin America.

In 1984 GWG laid off eighty-five people at the Edmonton laundry plant, and finishing for all clothing manufactured at Levi Strauss Canada and GWG plants in Edmonton, Stoney Creek, and Cornwall was consolidated in Brantford. Some of the finishing workers from Edmonton chose to relocate to Brantford along with the work, rather than lose their jobs. The cutters moved into the main plant in Edmonton.

GWG's workforce in Edmonton had declined from twelve hundred at its peak to five hundred. There were several reasons for the decline: materials and labour shortages, consolidation of work within Eastern plants, increase in imports from Levi Strauss plants in the developing world, the trend towards designer denims, and competition within the industry. After two decades of dominance, classic jeans fell out of fashion in the early 1980s, which led to a drop in production and layoffs in the manufacturing plants.

PARLEZ-VOUS FRANÇAIS?

GWG began to market its products to French Canadians in the 1960s as part of its efforts to broaden distribution throughout Canada. The company provided catalogue descriptions in both languages after 1965 and in 1980 GWG Limited officially changed its name to GWG Inc. in response to Bill 101 in Quebec, because "Inc." is the same in English or French. GWG introduced a few French-sounding brands: Cachet Cadet (1979), Femme Fit (1980), Poupounette (1980), and Pionnier (1980). GWG did not target a French-Canadian sensitivity, but marketed to specific genders, age groups, and interests.

GWG advertised extensively in English language newspapers and magazines until the 1970s, when it began to focus on radio and television ads and relied upon department stores' print ads to feature GWG products. The oldest French language newspaper ads found for GWG products date from 1976. Few GWG ads appeared in *Châtelaine*, the only fashion magazine widely available to Quebec women until the 1980s. GWG advertised men's Scrubbies in *Châtelaine*, recognizing that women often shopped for their husbands and sons. Other French magazine ads addressed girls and women of all ages.

GWG used the same advertising agency for both English and French language publicity, and advertisements were essentially the same in both languages. Ads were simply translated from English to French in Montreal, and francophone actors went to Toronto to tape commercials in French. In 1973 GWG translated its four Scrubbies radio ads featuring different musical genres into French. Gilles Girard, lead singer of the very popular group Les Classels, sang one version.

Most surviving French language advertising originated in the early 1980s. Two radio ads for Odyssey jeans were very different in style from earlier ads in that they did not use celebrity endorsement. The French version of the Bum Bums television ad was probably taped with English-speaking walk-on actors. There is no dialogue, only a few French words printed at the end, and the spirit and message of the ad work well in both languages.

A 1984 GWG television ad featured rising stars from Quebec, actors Serge Dupire and Marina Orsini. The ad may have been an adaptation of an English version; the use of recognizable young Quebec actors would have been more appealing to French Canadians. The ad played on the consumerist confusion that resulted from the explosion of designer jeans coming onto the market, and the amount of time wasted in choosing the right pair of jeans. GWG positioned itself as the simple choice for people with simple tastes who had no time to waste shopping for jeans.

GWG launched a major advertising campaign for its seventy-fifth anniversary in 1986, but if French language print ads were produced as a part of that campaign, they have not been found.

GWG Catalogue, 1968, RAM

A Woolworth ad in *Châtelaine*, May 1981, p. 148, mentions
Scrubbies. Bibliothèque et Archives nationales du Québec

GWG is mentioned under "Jeans corduroy et salopettes,
Boutique Les Amants," March 30, 1976. Bibliothèque et
Archives nationales du Québec

Ad for GWG filles, *Châtelaine*, April 1980, p. 103.
Bibliothèque et Archives nationales du Québec

Ad for GWGeans, *Châtelaine*,
September 1980, p. 91. Bibliothèque et
Archives nationales du Québec

Wayne Gretzky's, "I Grew Up in GWGs" campaign was translated and adapted for the French-Canadian market: "J'ai grandi avec GWG." Private Collection

GWG Catalogue, 1981. RAM

WAYNE GRETZKY REALLY DID GROW UP IN GWGS, 1981

In 1981 in an effort to attract a younger, hip audience, GWG was the first company anywhere to secure a celebrity endorsement from the young Wayne Gretzky, signing him for its, "I grew up in GWG's" campaign. Gretzky lived next door to Harry Lloyd, then manager of the Edward Street plant, and not only grew up in GWGs, but also, as Lloyd remembered, briefly worked there as a bundle boy. When Erin Braithwaite was in Junior High in St. Albert in the early 1980s, she focused her Career Day presentation on Wayne Gretzky. Unbeknownst to her, her teacher invited his friend, Gretzky's agent, to attend. After the presentation, he gave her this sweatshirt and photograph.

We grew up in GwG's

Many opposing players are convinced there's more than one Wayne Gretzky. Maybe there is!

Wayne is shown here wearing a few items from his GwG wardrobe including jeans, cords, shirt and a denim jacket. Look at the great fit.

The Great Wayne Gretzky scores again! And again! And again!

FIT WHERE IT COUNTS

I grew up in GwG's

Wayne Gretzky 99

"I Grew Up in GWG's" marketing materials including a sweatshirt worn by Wayne Gretzky, an autographed photograph, advertisement from an Edmonton Oiler's hockey program, and a store display card.
Lucie Heins, RAM

177

1986-2004

THE EDMONTON PLANT CONTINUED to function as a GWG plant until after the company's seventy-fifth anniversary in 1986 when it introduced the marketing campaign "History in the Making," capitalizing on GWG's longevity. Marketing materials gave no indication that GWG was part of Levis Strauss but shortly after the anniversary year, the plant became identified as Levi Strauss.

Workers from Twenty-Seven Different Countries

In 1986 93 percent of Levi's workers were immigrants; for 70 percent of them, their first job in Canada was at Levi's. The workforce in the Edmonton plant was predominantly Asian. The union tried to accommodate recent immigrants by holding meetings in English and Chinese. However, many immigrant women were reluctant to get involved in the union for various reasons: women who had been raised in cultural traditions that discouraged them from speaking out, or who came from

Teamwork
Levi's introduced various competitions to improve teamwork within the plant, increase efficiency, and reinforce the sense of community.
Courtesy of Barb Heath

countries where they had no political rights, or freedom to negotiate, were nervous about union involvement. Many simply lacked the time as they focused upon adapting to a new home, raising families, and earning as much money as possible to support extended families at home or bring family members to Canada. Some worked weekdays at the plant and nights or weekends at a second job.

Most former workers commented about the family environment at the plant. Many people enjoyed working there and meeting others living in similar circumstances. Immigrant women raised in cultures where men and women functioned in separate spheres found the female-dominated world of the plant familiar and comforting, given all of the changes taking place in their lives. Those who arrived in Edmonton at the same time, from the same country, supported one another. They understood the situation they had left behind in their homeland, and whether there were troubles or worries about relatives at home.

Working at GWG continued to be one of the best options for recent immigrants with limited use of English. The hours at the plant were better than those at jobs washing dishes in a restaurant or operating a small store, and they did not have to work weekends. When the plant offered day and night shifts, many women chose to work nights so they could be home for their children during the day and go to work when their husbands returned home from their day jobs. Others with school-aged children liked working during the day so they could be home when their children got home from school.

Those who became instructors and supervisors expressed appreciation for the opportunities for personal growth provided to them by GWG (later Levi Strauss), the English lessons, training, and opportunities for advancement. Workers

HISTORY IN THE MAKING

History in the Making, 1986

GWG's seventy-fifth anniversary campaign included billboards that said, "History in the Making," capitalizing on the company's long history. GWG introduced a number of new products in celebration. Jean Binette remembers that the focus of the celebrations was on the workers in each of the plants, not marketing GWG products. The Great Western Garment Company booklet, 1986.

Book Bag, 1986

The company reintroduced variations of the original logo after its seventy-fifth anniversary in 1986 to capitalize on the heritage value of the brand, some reintroducing the words Great Western Garment. Levi Strauss donated fabric to Tools for School, a United Way program, to make book bags. Lucie Heins, RAM, H08.17

Seventy-Fifth Anniversary, 1986

In 1986 GWG issued a small booklet celebrating the history of the company and held a huge banquet reminiscent of the annual union-management banquets of the past. They invited many retirees who had been long-term workers. A number of people worked at the plant for fifty years, their entire working lives. The company history does not mention that GWG belonged to Levi Strauss.

The Great Western Garment Company booklet, 1986.

Increasing Diversity

Edmonton's second-largest visible minority population is South Asian. In the late 1970s Indian, Indo-Trinidadian, and Indo-Fijian immigrants began working at the plant. Sadat Khan began working at GWG when she first arrived in Canada in 1977 and was still working there when the plant closed. Initially she found it difficult both physically and culturally. For example, she was told not to wear a sari because it could easily get caught up in machinery. In time, she came to enjoy the work and particularly the people with whom she worked.

Courtesy of Sadat Khan

appreciated small tokens, such as Plant Manager Jean Binette celebrating Chinese New Year by giving all employees a red envelope with a loonie inside.

Some immigrants who were well educated and had been professionals in their home countries found the work demeaning. Some did not enjoy the work — it was stressful trying to work as quickly as possible without making any mistakes. Like earlier immigrant workers, they felt they were lucky to have a job. Few used the word "sweatshop" when describing the working environment at Levi Strauss.

When Canadian-born Janet Cardinal, who had worked at the plant from 1962 to 1966, returned in 1988, she said there were "only eight Canadian girls working there." Cardinal recalled they used to use sign language to communicate with the others, and that when she was shop steward she had to ask the women to slow down when they would come to her

upset. "We always laughed about it...nobody got [so] upset that you couldn't understand them, we'd just work at it until we understood each other."

Although relations among diverse groups of people were generally good, workers initially tended to stick to their own cultural groups because of the language barrier and their focus on work. Giuseppina Tagliente, an Italian immigrant who worked at the plant from 1980 to 2004, commented that, "Because they were speaking the same language, and so most of the time they would stay together...they're more comfortable. Yeah, everybody like the East Indians they stay with East Indians, Italian with Italian, Chinese with Chinese, Portuguese with Portuguese, and so on."

There were occasionally conflicts between people from different countries. Binette observed that, "Like anything else, once you get to know people personally in a different

Elizabeth Kozma, 1997
Elizabeth Kozma had been a time engineer in a garment manufacturing company before she left Hungary in December 1956. She felt "very lucky" to be given permission to join her husband's family in Canada. They arrived in Halifax in January 1957 and came on to Edmonton. Her first job at GWG was attaching waistbands to pants for fifty cents an hour, sixteen dollars a week. Over the years, she learned a number of operations. She appreciated the opportunities that GWG and later Levi's provided. After twelve years on the production floor, she became a sewing instructor, and eventually a supervisor. She retired in 1997. Courtesy of Elizabeth Kozma

nationality, all of a sudden, they're no different than you are. It's just to get past that first wall, I guess. And a lot of history, from a lot of people in different countries, it doesn't change overnight."

Merlin Beharry, an Indo-Caribbean woman who worked at the plant from 1968 to 1999, said there was some conflict when non-European women started to become supervisors, but that, "Whatever negative vibes that came our way, did not come from the workers. It came from some of the supervisors, the European supervisors. We are treading on sacred territory now. There was Kulminder [Bolina], there was another girl from India who's no longer here in Edmonton, and myself. They were there years before us. This was their domain. I don't know if I'm using the right word, but that's what it amounted to."

Occupational Health and Safety

Awareness of health and safety issues in industrial environments increased throughout the second half of the twentieth century. The company introduced preventive measures as it became more aware of risks to workers' health and safety. It became a better, safer place to work. Chris Tigeris initially worked full-time as the occupational health nurse from 1986, until she had a baby in 1989 and returned to work part-time, later job-sharing with Barb Heath, from 1993 until the plant closed.

The role of the nurse had changed significantly by this time. The nurse was no longer responsible for hiring or other human resources functions, although she still did hearing and eye tests for new employees. She was responsible for helping injured workers and for educating workers and inspecting the plant to try to prevent injuries. As the industry learned more about ergonomics, the company taught the workers how to adjust their chairs, and made cushions to support their backs.

There continued to be few major injuries in the plant. However, some workers continued to suffer from various long-term conditions. Eighty percent of the injuries were repetitive strain injuries — particularly to the elbows, wrists, shoulders. Heath said, "A lot of them were afraid and thought they might get fired if they came to us. Sometimes they'd come and be crying. They'd be so desperate by the time they came to us, they had a very bad injury."

The nurses became involved in transferring machine operators from one operation to another. The union began to allow operators to learn more than one operation. This reduced the number of repetitive strain injuries. It also meant that the company became more efficient because they lost less time switching from producing one garment to another. This led to the Edmonton plant being the most efficient Levi's plant.

The nurses worked with the union to allow injured workers, rather than workers with the most seniority, to be given priority in transferring to different machines. Sometimes they recommended modified work hours for employees returning after an injury. Unfortunately, the problems were so serious for some operators that they could not ever return to work. The nurses monitored absenteeism and assisted with Workmen's Compensation and disability claims. They taught first aid to workers in the plant. There were always more people certified with first aid than required.

They introduced protective glasses in the mid-1980s, and earplugs for all workers in the mid-1990s. Previously only those working on particularly noisy machines wore earplugs, but as each new automated machine was introduced, the overall noise level in the plant increased. The company provided different types of gloves depending upon the machinery and the type of fabric being cut or sewn.

Most workers stopped wearing dust masks in the early 1980s because there was less lint in the factory and dust was no longer considered a hazard. Although the workers sometimes coughed up blue phlegm from the denim, the nurses could not find any references to it being dangerous. After the finishing plant closed, chemicals were no longer a problem.

Chris Tigeris described a Lunch and Learn program she introduced to provide health and wellness information to the workers. "We'd do an English one, and frequently we'd get a translator to come in and do a Chinese one. Frequently, we'd get a Punjabi interpreter in to do the same presentation again in Punjabi." Some of the translators were sewing instructors, which was helpful, because they could present safety information while they were training workers.

As well as safety in the workplace, they addressed women's health issues, the importance of regular pap smears, breast self-examinations, and mammograms, for example. It was the only company in Alberta that ever had technologists come on site to do mammograms because of the large number of women working at the plant. Many of them would not have taken the test on their own.

GWG also collaborated with the Alberta Motor Association (AMA) because the workers had a high accident rate. Often workers would car pool, so if they were in an accident four workers would be late or absent. The AMA did a series of lunch-hour presentations about traffic safety and prevention of traffic accidents.

Barb Heath said that,

> Normally in my job now, what takes two seconds would take ten minutes or longer, trying to explain. Even things like vision tests. When they first came, we did an assessment to make sure they could see. These ladies would come, sometimes

having been in Canada for only two weeks. They were so nervous coming for this medical [exam], I don't know what they thought I was going to do to them. They wanted this job really badly, and I think they thought I could fail them and not give them the job. We'd try to make them feel at ease, but they were very nervous.

Nurses sometimes used pictures rather than words to explain potential injuries: "[We] put up pictures of a person, and then shade in the area that might get sore if they were working on that job. So they could just see, even if they couldn't read, just by looking at the picture. If the left shoulder was shaded in the picture, then they knew they'd better have strong left shoulder muscles." They also encouraged culturally appropriate practices to avoid repetitive strain injuries. "Early in the morning, especially in the summer, out on the lawn in front of the building, you'd see ladies that were doing Tai Chi." Exercising out of doors is common in China and a practice that transferred to Edmonton.

Working with the immigrant women was a great learning experience for the language teachers and nurses. Tigeris said, "I always found it interesting how the cultures intermingled. A Chinese baby would be born, and there'd be some East Indian food brought in." Heath noted, "If someone had an injury, we'd see an East Indian lady walking in with a Chinese medicine patch on. It really surprised me when I first started, because I had worked at another company where there [were] immigrant workers. There wasn't that family atmosphere like there was at Levi's. It was just a different place to work."

Workers in the Brantford finishing plant faced different occupational hazards than did the operators in Edmonton. In September 1997 a chlorine tank blasted through the roof of the plant. Fortunately, damage was minimal; although five workers were sent to the hospital, none were seriously injured. The plant reopened the next day. This explosion followed a sulphuric acid spill in January 1990 that created potentially explosive hydrogen gas, and the accidental mixing of chlorine and an unknown chemical in 1992, a similar incident to the 1997 explosion.

English in the Workplace

With workers speaking so many different languages, and translators conveying information, Binette was never sure that the workers were hearing the same message he was speaking. Therefore, in 1986, he contracted Virginia Sauve, who was at the time a graduate student working on a thesis about English in the workplace, to introduce a new English in the Workplace program in order to improve communication and efficiency in the Edmonton plant. In a two-week period, she and Beverly Walker, who later coordinated the program, assessed the English level of more than 500 of the 735 workers for whom English was not their first language, and developed the program. Initially, the company gave priority to workers with the lowest level of English language skills.

The program operated for seventeen years. Workers received six instructional hours a week, with classes after work and on Saturday mornings. The program provided both language and literacy classes, with ten to twelve people in each language class, and eight or nine in each literacy class. At its peak, they offered sixteen classes a week. Unlike the program offered in the 1960s, there was no limit to the number of hours. Like the earlier program, it was initially funded by the Government. After a few years, the company covered the cost, but the teachers never worked directly for Levi Strauss.

The company used the English in the Workplace classes to convey important information to the workers, such as

English in the Workplace

Participants in the English classes got together for social events as well, such as dim sum, cooking classes, and field trips. One picnic at the Devonian Gardens was particularly memorable. They met in the parking lot at 9:00 a.m. on a Saturday morning so those without cars could get a ride and everyone could drive out together. But the women invited their family and friends along so they formed a long convoy of cars with Virginia Sauve at the head and Beverly Walker bringing up the rear to make sure no one got lost. About 150 people attended: husbands, children, grandmothers, along with big coolers of food.

Courtesy of Beverly Walker

changes in company policy or health and safety information. The union used the classes to explain meeting agendas and the collective agreement.

The workers learned much more than English. The teachers answered questions about the community, explained notices from their children's schools, organized field trips, provided resources, and even staged a mock election to encourage workers to vote! The ability to communicate more effectively gave the participants more confidence both at work and in the community, in intimidating situations like parent-teacher interviews, doctors' appointments, and media interviews. One participant told her English teacher, "'We feel like a frog in the well,'... now they were out of the well."

Workers often raised any concerns they had about their work with their language teachers. If there were any serious problems the teachers alerted management, but usually they helped people to resolve their issues. They created strong bonds of friendship through the classes. Virginia Sauve explained that "these became little communities...we go to their weddings, we go to their anniversary celebrations, we go to the baptisms." She remembered the time when a woman "brought her first child, she just arrived with her baby, her husband, a bunch of her friends, and a box of food one Saturday morning for the three-month party that they do with babies, you know. If a baby lives for three months in the Chinese custom, that's when they celebrate the birth."

Sauve recalled:

> Because so many of the Chinese women took the program...some of the other groups decided this was a Chinese program. It wasn't and they—the women—some of them would speak Chinese in the classes, which the other women hated, so you had to be really committed....The Vietnamese

women tended to learn Chinese while they were working in the plant because it just made their lives easier.…When they came in they might only speak Vietnamese, but boy when they left, they spoke Chinese too.…But the Indian women didn't come to the classes and that's unfortunate because while their verbal skills — most of them — were quite good, many of them didn't have literacy, and they missed a wonderful opportunity…and then we'd have some Filipina women, Portuguese. We had several Portuguese women. There was one class that was actually predominantly Portuguese.

The workers were initially paid to take the classes, but Sauve noted:

> The women were terrified because they were being paid, that they were going to lose the program, because it was so much money that was being spent — way more than was actually spent on the program itself, was spent on paying the people to be there. So it was actually the women who asked not to be paid, and indeed we lost a few students — I'd say maybe 15 to 20 percent — of the students when they weren't getting paid decided they didn't really want to come, because most of these women work more than one job, and they'll do anything to earn more money. They're supporting huge, extended families, some of them still there waiting to be sponsored.

Susan Bui, who emigrated from Vietnam in 1985 and started working at the factory right away, said that with two children under two, she and her husband also had second jobs to sponsor their family members: "So, I have to go to work on Saturday and Sunday. So, I had to take another job, and my husband had to take another job, to earn enough money to sponsor nine people."

The Edmonton plant had a much higher proportion of immigrant workers than did the Brantford plant. By 1990, 40 percent of the workforce in Brantford was made up of immigrant workers. GWG offered English as a Second Language classes at both plants, in Brantford, too, with a focus on safety manuals, union contracts, and other work-related material. Workers contributed half an hour of their lunch breaks for lessons and the company contributed half an hour in wages. Initially run by Mohawk College, the Brant County Board of Education later provided classes.

Levis Strauss Absorbed GWG

Soon after the seventy-fifth anniversary in 1986, the company became known as a Levi Strauss plant, rather than GWG. Levi Strauss closed nearly sixty of its American plants in the 1980s and began shifting production overseas.

Rumours of the Edmonton plant closing escalated. During negotiations with the union in 1990, management from Toronto said that Levi's was threatening to close the plant. Anne Ozipko decided to go to a Levi Strauss board meeting in San Francisco to find out for herself. As a shareholder, she received notification of the meetings. Levi's gave workers shares in the company after they had worked there for fifteen years, five shares for every five years worked.

After the meeting, Ozipko said to President Peter Haas, "'Our people are upset that there is some talk about you closing our plant.' He says, 'No, we're not planning to close your plant.' He says, 'Your plant is the best plant we've got.'" So when she resumed negotiations and was told, "'This is

No Sweat: What's in a Label?
The Ethical Trading Action Group proposed labelling regulations to allow consumers to tell whether companies were producing apparel under decent conditions or under sweatshop conditions, much as the "union made" label once did. Eighty percent of Canadians support providing labels indicating where clothing is made. However, a "Made in Canada" label is no guarantee that goods were not made under sweatshop conditions. There are sweatshops in Canada and the incidence of homework, clothing manufactured in homes rather than factories, is on the rise. These GWGs were made in Bangladesh. Lucie Heins, RAM

OPPOSITE: **Levi's Production Floor, 2004**
By the time the Edmonton plant closed in February 2004, only Levi's jeans and Dockers pants were made locally; seventeen thousand pairs were manufactured daily.
Photography by Andrena Shaw, *Ground Zero Productions*

what I've got to offer, and if you don't take it they're going to close the plant.' I said, 'Like hell they are!' He looks at me, 'Who told you?' I said, 'I got it from the horse's mouth, from Peter Haas.'…So I said, 'You can take your junk and go back home where you came from, and come back with something that you're going to offer us.' And he did."

However, the company continued to shift production to subcontractors in the developing world. In 1991 Levi Strauss faced a scandal involving its subsidiaries on the Northern Mariana Islands, a United States commonwealth. Levi's marketed jeans as being made in the USA when, in fact, they were made by Chinese workers in sweatshop conditions: sub-minimum wages, seven-day workweeks with twelve-hour shifts, and poor living conditions. The subcontractor, Tan Holdings Corporation, paid more than $9 million in restitution to twelve hundred workers, the largest fine in United States' labour history. Levi Strauss said they had no idea what was going on inside the plant. Levi's severed ties with the Tan family and introduced international standards for contractors to ensure its products were manufactured under acceptable working conditions.

The End of Piecework
The plant marked a major turning point in 1993, when the company stopped paying by piecework and introduced a quota system with automated tracking. GWG had modified the ticket system in 1984 so that each bundle had a ticket with a bar code that the operators had to scan. With the new system, the company tracked production rates automatically.

Initially, workers were offered a 5 percent incentive if they reached their quota. Supervisor Kulminder Bolina, who worked at the plant from 1973 to 2004 said, "Then it went to teamwork. If somebody's behind, the other team has to help. A team member has to help the other person over there. So they have to work together." If all the work was of good quality, they received a bonus.

Wages were set based upon the difficulty of the operation: the harder the job, the higher the rate. Janet Cardinal remembered, "When I worked on buttonholes, I did sixty pair of pants and I had to do fifty bundles a day to make 100 percent. On a harder job, like when I was doing the front pockets and to topstitch the fly, I only had to do nine bundles a day. And then when I was doing hemming, I had to do seventeen bundles a day, so it all depended on the difficulty of the job, how much you got paid per bundle." The highest paid operators were earning fourteen dollars an hour, more than any other garment workers in North America.

Levi's still monitored production very closely, and there was still a lot of pressure to work very quickly to complete the required number of operations per hour. Even though the possibility of closure was always in the back of people's minds, they continued to introduce new practices right up until the end. By the time the plant closed in 2004, Levi's reduced the amount of time it took to manufacture a pair of jeans to seven and a half minutes.

Great Western Garment had attempted to move from piecework to hourly wages in the 1940s; however, operators whose wages dropped resisted the change and they reverted to piecework. For many years, management was concerned that because many of the operators did not understand English, they would not understand the shift to piecework. Operators with limited English were afraid of the new system, but the English in the Workplace classes helped them to understand and adjust to the new system.

In 1994 the United Garment Workers of America merged with the United Food and Commercial Workers International Union (UFCW), thinking there was more strength in numbers. The UFCW established an Apparel, Garment, and Textile Workers Council. This change did not alter relationships between the union and management. Working conditions and wages were very good and the union was very keenly aware of the financial difficulties Levi's faced, as well as the competition from workers in developing nations. The North American Free Trade Agreement (NAFTA), introduced in 1993, impacted the Canadian and American garment manufacturing industries by making it easier for manufacturers to move jobs to lower-cost Mexico, leading some manufacturers that remained to lower wages in order to compete. The union's focus became holding on to Canadian jobs.

In 1993 the company cut operations by 40 percent in Brantford and introduced a work sharing program for six weeks, with employees working three days a week and being laid off for the other two. Production increased again in 1995, and Levi's expanded the Brantford finishing plant. With the additional 2,040 square metres of space, the workforce increased to 468 workers, making the plant the second-largest employer in the city, operating twenty-four hours a day, seven days a week. However, workers at the Stoney Creek plant went on strike for a month in 1995, resulting in an extended layoff at the Brantford plant.

Globalization was only one of the challenges faced by Levi's. Levi's were more expensive than other classic jeans, and less fashionable than designer jeans. With a growing demand for designer jeans and store labels in the mid-1990s, the popularity of Levi's continued to decline.

Levi Strauss introduced profit sharing with its employees. In 1996 the company offered an unusual incentive to employees: a chance to share a $16 million prize under a Global Success Sharing Plan, a one-time cash bonus equal to one year's salary if the company met its target of $7.6 billion by the end of its 2002 fiscal year. Unfortunately, although the company did meet its target, the cash was somehow not forthcoming.

Levi Strauss closed eleven plants in the United States in November 1997, laying off nearly sixty-four hundred employees in four states. The layoffs did not immediately affect Canadian plants, and the company insisted that it would not shift manufacturing jobs to its plants in Mexico or Southeast Asia. At the time, the Canadian plants produced 215,000 units a week, 10.2 million units a year. In 1998 Levi's laid off two hundred workers in the Brantford finishing plant when the Cornwall plant was shut down for fifty-eight days, and the Stoney Creek plant for twenty-three days. These workers were not rehired. At 250 employees, the workforce remained half its former size.

In September 1998 Levi Strauss closed two more plants in Texas, and in February 1999, another eleven North American plants, laying off 5,900 workers, including 479

The Final Step in Making Jeans, 2004
FACING PAGE: Parduman Atwal pulls buttons through buttonholes, a motion she did 2,700 times a day. Most operators performed the same task day in, day out, for many years.
Photograph by Andrena Shaw, *Ground Zero Productions*

Automated Production, 2004

ABOVE: In contrast to the early years, by 2004 safety had become an important issue. Operators wore earplugs, gloves or taped fingers, rubber thimbles, and safety glasses. Some wore dust masks. Many operators wore aprons and sleeves to protect their clothing from lint. Here, Qui Dien operates a machine that attaches the riser to the back legs then piles the pant legs on a cart to take to the next operator.

Photograph by Andrena Shaw, *Ground Zero Productions*

World's Largest Jeans, 2001

When Edmonton hosted the IAAF World Championships in Athletics in 2001, workers at the plant made the world's largest jeans. Because the workforce was from around the world, they wanted to welcome the athletes. Unfortunately, the event organizers saw it as an ambush, not a welcome, and complained to the city that Levi's was associating itself with the games without paying a sponsorship fee. The jeans were eight storeys high, thirty times the size of a regular pair of pants, and weighed 246 kilograms. The zipper was four metres long, the inseam twenty-four metres, and the waist nineteen metres. They took three hundred hours to make. Courtesy of Kim Ngo

at the Cornwall plant, to cut production and offset falling sales. The closure of the Cornwall plant resulted in the loss of 101 workers at the finishing centre in Brantford because of the reduction in production.

Levi's also considered shutting down the Edmonton plant, but in the end it was spared because of its efficiency. The Edmonton plant produced a wider range of products including the company's profitable Dockers and Levi's brands. Workers discussed rumours of the possibility of closure at a meeting of all staff, and they remained anxious for their jobs when later that year the company laid off seventy-seven people at the Edmonton plant.

Edmonton continued to focus on improving production efficiency. In 1998 a new $850,000 laser cutting unit, developed by Edmonton's Lacent Technologies Inc. was installed at the plant. Chee Luck Mah, who had worked at the plant since 1963, first as a cloth spreader and then as a cutter, said that the transition to the laser printer was not entirely smooth, but in the end it reduced labour costs significantly. The machine spread and cut the fabric and reduced the time required to cut pieces for twelve hundred pairs of pants from twelve to three and a half hours.

In 1998 Levi Strauss licensed the GWG brand to Montreal manufacturer Jack Spratt so it could focus on its Levi's and Dockers brands. When this contract expired in 2001, Levi Strauss resumed production of GWGs in Edmonton and Stoney Creek. Levi Strauss also introduced a new logo that featured the name "Great Western Garment Company" in a circle with the letters "GWG" in the centre, a nod to the history of the company.

When Edmonton entertained the world at the 2001 IAAF World Championships in Athletics, the 530 workers from the twenty-seven nations represented in the workforce at the Edmonton plant wanted to do something to celebrate the multicultural plant and to welcome athletes. Binette said that they got into the *Guinness Book of Records* for the largest pair of blue jeans in the world. The production was a significant feat; however, the city did not share in the enthusiasm and ordered that they take them down because games organizers found the sight unattractive.

In 2002 LS&CO. closed six more American plants, eliminating another thirty-three hundred jobs. At that time it introduced the less expensive Signature brand at Wal-Mart. However, the Signature brand was not as successful as anticipated and made consumers reluctant to pay premium prices for Levi's sold elsewhere. Following on seven years of consecutive financial losses, LS&CO. posted its largest loss ever — US$349 million. The impact of the North American Free Trade Agreement was felt throughout the clothing industry — Canada's sixth largest manufacturing sector — as ten thousand jobs were lost in other garment manufacturing companies.

Levi's 150th Anniversary, 2003
When Levi's celebrated its 150th anniversary in 2003, the company developed a travelling exhibit that was installed in various shopping centres, including the Eaton Centre in downtown Toronto. Courtesy of Ian Cole

"I Saw My Manager Cry"

In May 2003 LS&CO. celebrated its 150th anniversary with an international travelling exhibition. However, the celebration was short-lived. That fall the company announced that it would close its remaining plants in North America: three in Canada and two in the United States. LS&CO. was the last major clothing company to stop manufacturing in North America, a step others had taken twenty years before.

A number of factors impacted Levi's flagging profitability in the 1980s and 1990s and led to the closure: periods of economic recession and weak management; competition from non-unionized plants and the lower cost of labour in developing nations; changes in retailing; the flattening of the classic jeans market; and inability to connect with the youth

market or find a niche in the fashion jeans market. Levi's sales had dropped 40 percent since 1996. Levi's focused on cutting production costs and Canada's free trade policies hastened the loss of garment manufacturing jobs. When the plants closed in March 2004, 1,180 workers lost their jobs in Canada: 231 at the finishing centre in Brantford, 461 in Stoney Creek, and 488 in Edmonton. Levi's sold the assets of the Brantford and Edmonton plants to single buyers in the developing world. The Edmonton plant has since been torn down.

Levi Strauss treated the workers as fairly as possible during the closure. The company had learned over the years about the importance of public relations surrounding such an announcement. In 1990 Levi's had closed a non-unionized plant in San Antonio without notice and with minimal severance pay. Workers engaged in protests, hunger strikes, and acts of civil disobedience to call attention to the company's lack of corporate responsibility. As a result, they won a better severance package and retraining support, and damaged Levi's image.

When the Edmonton, Brantford, and Stoney Creek plants were closed, Levi's minimized damage by announcing a generous severance package, career counselling, and retraining, as well as philanthropic donations to local charities as part of its exit strategy. Few, however, found comparable jobs elsewhere.

Although Binette had retired and been replaced by Nancy Wong, he returned to the plant to help with the closure. Binette said that, although it was a very difficult situation, "The company went out of their way and did things that, in my personal opinion, a company that was making good money probably wouldn't even do, and that's how committed that GWG, and Levi's in their days, were to the people. And they've always been that way."

Working with Economic Development Edmonton, Levi Strauss initiated the "Levi's 488 Project" to help workers find new jobs through a job fair. Unfortunately, many workers did not have the English language skills necessary to easily transfer to another type of work with comparable salary and benefits. Four months after the plant closed, only 105 former employees had found new jobs; 51 were retired, 137 were enrolled in retraining programs, 66 were actively looking for work, and 129 were still thinking about what to do next.

Many former workers in Edmonton have discussed the sadness they felt at the time. Kim Ngo remembered, "When we heard the announcement that they were going to close, everybody cried. I cried. At nighttime I said, 'Is it a dream? I hope it is a dream.' We did not want to lose it. Some of us even

think, could we reduce the wage so that we all can stay? We all connect one another. I saw my manager cry, we cried."

Sadat Khan remembered, "We share our sadness, our happiness together. Somebody listen to us, like close friends. That one I miss. Now we are alone.... Sometimes I cry when I remember. Still I am dreaming about Levi's, that I'm working there. That one I miss. It's very good time of my life, twenty-five years. Very good time."

Then Edmonton mayor Bill Smith said the decision to close the plant was "almost inevitable in the global economy." Was the closure of the plant inevitable? Perhaps by 2004, it was. The 1961 decision to sell the majority of GWG to Levi Strauss, and, by the mid-1980s, the integration of GWG operations into a huge multinational firm took the ultimate decision about the future of the plant out of local hands. Had it remained in local ownership, it might have been able to compete in the fashion denim market, where price point is less significant.

A Lasting Legacy

Throughout its history, GWG was a very innovative company. GWG set standards in management, labour relations, and working conditions. By 1917 Local 120 was reputed to be the first garment manufacturing union in North America to gain the eight-hour-day and forty-hour-week. In the 1960s GWG worked closely with retailers to develop a unique inventory control system. In 1965 GWG was the first Alberta company to partner with the government to provide training. In terms of products, in the 1920s, GWG was the first company in Canada to use pre-shrunk denim. In 1972 GWG developed Scrubbies, the original pre-washed jeans.

GWG thrived in its first fifty years through innovation, flexibility (something that is difficult to achieve in a highly engineered plant or a huge bureaucracy), and cooperation with labour and the local community. Its accomplishments are particularly significant given that GWG was the only major garment manufacturing company west of Winnipeg.

The importance of the Great Western Garment Company to the development of Edmonton as a city should not be underestimated. Because the factory provided opportunities for working women with little or no English, it became a major employer of immigrants in the postwar period. Many immigrants who came to Edmonton hoping for a better life for their children found work at GWG. The presence of GWG, and later Levi Strauss, allowed them to stay in the city rather than move elsewhere in Canada to find work. In some cases, the parents returned to their home countries when circumstances improved there; although, their children and grandchildren remain in Canada and may be found in all walks of life in Edmonton today.

GWG CATALOGUES

The earliest GWG catalogues that have been found are Fall/Winter 1938/39 and Spring/Summer 1939. Catalogues featured fashion illustrations rather than photographs, although illustrators often used photographs of staff and family members for reference to help them visualize how the clothing appeared while being worn and to create an accurate image. Sometimes the same illustration was used for several years and for magazine advertisements and in-store advertisements, as well as for the catalogues.

The 1940/41 GWG Catalogue was a wholesale catalogue used by stores to place their orders. The staff at the store that originally used this catalogue wrote in code in the page margins to keep track of orders. The 1942 *Household Handbook* included recipes, housekeeping hints, and breeding records as well as clothing illustrations. GWG encouraged customers to keep the catalogue visible by printing a 1943 calendar on the back and providing a string to hang it in a convenient place. From 1944 to 1949, GWG published almanacs with photographs of the GWG factory, horoscopes, and other information. The 1947 Almanac included tips on how to remake military issue clothing for civilian wear. GWG advertised the almanacs in magazines and asked readers to write to GWG to request a copy.

The 1950 GWG Catalogue was a large, fifty-page catalogue of fashion illustrations and retail prices. By 1959 the catalogue was reduced to twelve pages in a horizontal format that was used for the next decade. The catalogues were again given to customers by local dealers, with the dealers' names printed on the cover.

In 1968 the catalogues were bilingual, printed in English and French, and returned to a vertical format. The cover of the 1968 GWG Catalogue says, "Get in the color picture with GWG," suggesting that was the first year that photographs replaced fashion illustrations. With faster cameras, less expensive film, and electronic lighting, illustrative art lost its edge. Colour photography and four-colour lithography became the norm for magazine advertising and catalogues.

GWG Catalogue Fall/Winter 1938/39.

GWG Wholesale Catalogue, 1940/41.

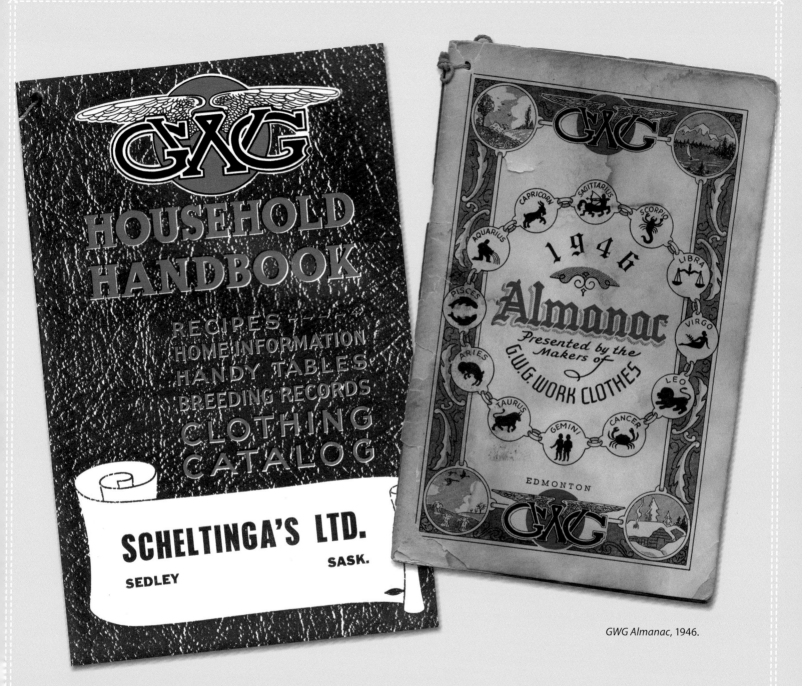

GWG Household Handbook, 1942.

GWG Almanac, 1946.

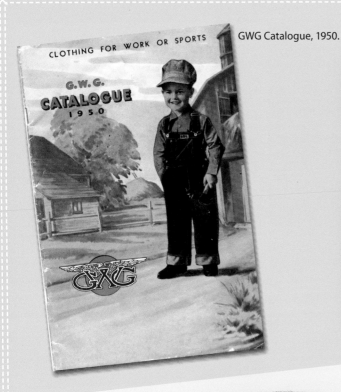

GWG Catalogue, 1950.

GWG Catalogue, 1959.

GWG Catalogue, 1960.

GWG Catalogue, 1965.

GWG Catalogue, 1970. RAM

GWG Catalogue, 1968. RAM

GWG Catalogue, 1980. RAM

HOW TO MAKE A PAIR OF JEANS

Once the fabric was cut, stacked in bundles of sixty pieces and tied with the order number, style, size, and quantity, it was ready to be constructed. Labels were attached to the inside of the waistbands. Zippers were cut, sliders attached, then the zippers attached to the front leg.

1 Miao Deng sewed and topstitched the left zipper fly.

2 The front pockets were put in position, then Li Chan He topstitched the front pocket and right fly using a single needle machine. The left and right pocket pieces were sewn to the front pant legs and the pockets bags were stitched around the bottom.

3 The right fly was serged, then Hui Fang Feng topstitched the fly and joined the pant legs at the crotch.

4 Lien Tran bar tacked the front pockets.

5 The decorative stitching on the back pocket was applied automatically, and Mai Mui Wong applied the back pocket to the pant leg.

6 The riser was attached to the back legs then put on a cart to be taken to the next operator. Ai Yi Yan sewed the back seam using a 2-needle flat felling machine.

7 The fronts and backs were joined, ensuring both bundles were from the same dye. Xin (Allan) Qiang Huang serged the outer leg seam to keep it from fraying.

8 Amandeep Gill turned and stacked the jeans.

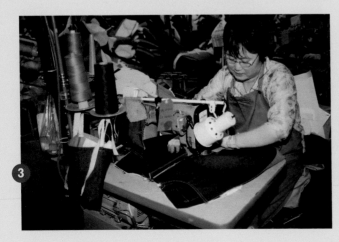

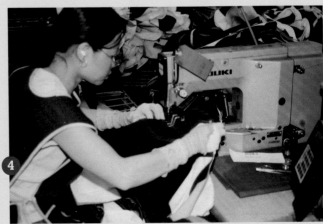

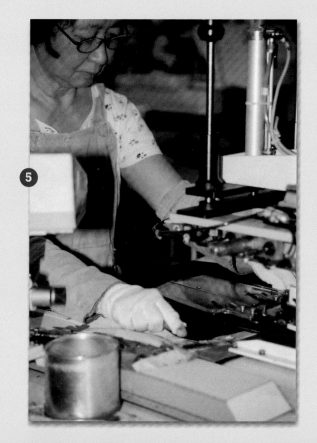

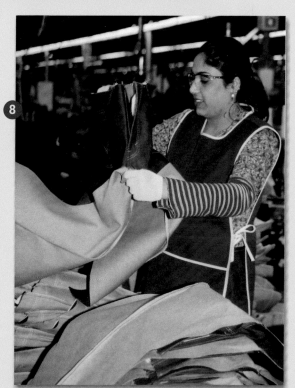

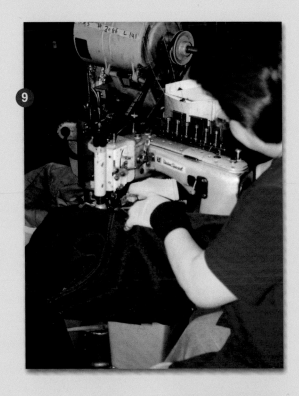

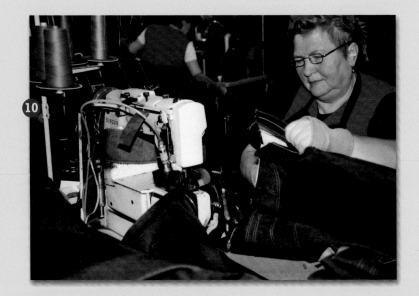

9   Chi Tran performed the most difficult operation, sewing the flat felled inseam. She had to gauge the 3/16" seam allowance, and match the pant legs at both hems and the crotch.

10   Once the pant legs were joined and the inseam sewn, Halina Gradzi attached the waistband.

11   Bernadette Medeiros made the buttonholes and attached the buttons. The buttonholer and riveter were placed side by side so the operator could use both hands and do two pairs at a time.

12   Michela Colangelo operated two machines, feeding fabric through one while the other sewed a supply of belt loops to be attached to the waistband. Each pair of jeans had five to seven belt loops, depending upon the waist size. The belt loops were tacked in place.

13   Parminder Nijjar attached four rivets on the pocket corners using a machine with a light that showed where to put the rivets.

14   Mai Fung Wong hemmed the pant legs.

15   Yuan Ai Feng attached the leather label to the waistband. She needed to be careful to attach the correct style and size of label.

16   Parduman Atwal closed the zipper and buttoned the pants for folding and packing.

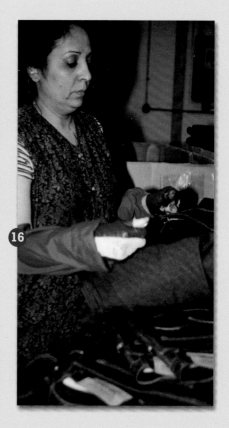

All Photographs by Andrena Shaw,
Ground Zero Productions, February 2004.

NOTES ON SOURCES

Relatively little has been published about the Canadian garment industry. What has been written focuses on the larger manufacturing centres: Montreal, Toronto, and Winnipeg; on the more radical unions: the Amalgamated Clothing Workers of America (ACWA) and the International Ladies Garment Workers Union (ILGWU); on dressmaking more so than men's clothing; and on themes such as sweatshops, labour unrest, homework, ethnicity, and gender issues. This work has been useful in providing contrast to the situation at GWG. As well, local and regional histories and labour histories have provided useful context. A number of publications tell various aspects of the history of Levi Strauss & Co., but not its relationship to GWG.

REPOSITORIES

Alberta Registries, Corporate Registries, Edmonton

Archives of Ontario, Toronto

Bibliothèque et Archives nationales du Québec, Montreal

Brant Historical Society, Brantford, Ontario

Brantford Public Library

Calgary Exhibition and Stampede Archives

Canadian Intellectual Property Office, Gatineau, Quebec

City of Edmonton Archives (COEA)

Corporate Registry, Information Services Corporation, Regina, Saskatchewan

Edmonton Public Library, Heritage Room

Georgia State University Archives, Special Collections and Archives

Glenbow Archives, Calgary (GA)

GWG Archives, Great Northern Apparel, now LS&CO., Canada, Richmond Hill, Ontario

Library and Archives Canada, Ottawa (LAC)

Manitoba Archives, Winnipeg

Manitoba Consumer and Corporate Affairs Companies Office, Winnipeg

McCord Museum, Montreal

Ministry of Government Services, Toronto, Ontario

Provincial Archives of Alberta, Edmonton (PAA)

Reynolds-Alberta Museum, Wetaskiwin (Reynolds)

Royal Alberta Museum, Edmonton (RAM)

Saskatoon City Archives

Saskatoon Public Library, Local History Room

University of Saskatchewan Archives, Saskatoon

Western Development Museum, Saskatoon (WDM)

OTHER PRIMARY SOURCES

GWG corporate records in private collections

Magazines and newspapers

Oral history and correspondence with former employees

INDEX

A

A. Bradshaw and Sons Ltd. 160, 161
Act for the Protection of Persons
 Employed in Factories, Shops and
 Office Buildings. *See* Factories Act
Act to Provide a Minimum Wage for
 Women 35
advertising 15, 22, 28, 30, 31, 33, 34, 35, 36,
 37, 55, 56, 102, 109, 115, 119, 120, 121,
 123, 124, 140, 142, 146, 152, 166, 171,
 175
 in-store 195
 magazine 195
 newspaper 173
 radio 164, 173
 television 164, 173
Aircraft Repair Ltd. 98, 105
Alberta Beach AB 44
Alberta Blue Cross Plan 114
Alberta Federation of Labour (AFL) 20,
 30, 38, 39, 131, 133
 conventions 38, 39, 40, 134, 152
Alberta Garment Manufacturers Ltd. 24
Alberta Hotel 19, 54
Alberta Labor News 22, 23, 33, 35, 36
Alberta Motor Association (AMA) 184
Alberta War Labor Board 99
Allen, Helen 88
Allen, Valerie 121
Amalgamated Clothing Workers of
 America (ACWA) 20, 30, 162
 Local 551 160, 168
American Federation of Labor (AFL) 20,
 39, 131
apprentices 21, 39
aprons, truckers' leg 127
Army & Navy Department Stores 117

B

Arndt, Ruth 88
assembly line 53, 98, 165
Atwal, Parduman 190, 202

Baldwin, Peter 121
Banff AB 134
Bangladesh 17, 188
Beaudoin, Juliette 100
Bedard, Max 21, 30, 59, 124
Beharry, Merlin 183
belt buckles 140, 145
Bentall Engineering 167
Berg, Carl 99, 117
Bill 101 173
Binette, Jean 163, 172, 181, 182, 185, 193,
 194
blouses 24, 39
Bolina, Kulminder 183, 189
book bags 181
Braithwaite, Erin 177
brand names. *See* type of garment
Brantford ON 17, 160, 161, 162, 163, 164,
 167, 168, 169, 172, 185, 187, 190, 192,
 193, 194
Bridgewater, Brenda 164
Britannia 164
British Army 30
British Trade Union Congress 131
Broad, Anne (Baranyk) 125, 133, 134, 151
Broad, Bill 134
Brownlee, Ralph 116
Bui, Susan 187
bundle boys 21, 34, 94, 102, 177
bundle girls 34, 93, 94, 102
"Bunkhouse Bunch Member" 145, 202

button flies 110
buttons 99, 110, 113, 190, 202
 trouser 110

C

Caledonian Department Store 33
Calgary AB 16, 39, 119, 125, 134, 140, 152
Calgary Exhibition and Stampede 93
Cameron, Alf 92
Camrose AB 160
Canada Manpower Centre 159
Canada Savings Bonds 98
Canada-US Free Trade Agreement (FTA)
 165
Canadian Cottons 15, 54, 59
Canadian Finals Rodeo 140, 144, 171
Canadian Garment Manufacturers'
 Association 93
Canadian Intellectual Property Office 64
Canadian Trades and Labour Congress
 (CTLC) 131, 134, 153
 conventions 134
 Union Label Trades Department 134
Cardinal, Janet 158, 182, 189
carpal tunnel syndrome 131
carpenters 22
Chan, Mee 156
chaps 140
Chatelaine 171
Châtelaine 173, 174, 175
childcare 98
children's wear 17, 124, 146, 172
China 161, 185
Chinese Immigration Act 156
Cluett, Sanford L. 59
Colangelo, Michela 202

Combines Investigation Act 169
Commonwealth Air Training Plan 105
Commonwealth Printing 119
Community Involvement Teams 169
Compensation Board 157
competition 114, 133, 152, 161-162, 165,
        171, 172, 190, 193
    American 165
    Asian 133
    Chinese 162
    Hong Kong 162
    Japanese 133, 162
Consumer and Corporate Affairs 35, 39
Cornwall ON 15, 17, 54, 165, 167, 172,
        190, 192
Cosgrave, Doug 140
Country Guide 47, 55, 62, 64, 67, 68, 70, 71,
        72, 73, 76, 79, 102, 112, 137, 139, 140,
        141, 142, 143, 148, 149
Courtney Manufacturing 24, 39
coveralls 169
    Red Strap 51
cowboys 124, 140, 146
cutters 21, 26, 27, 34, 42, 92, 93, 94, 106,
        163, 172, 192
cutting room 26, 151

D
Daniels, Howard D. 160, 161
Davis, Stu 140, 141
daycare 164
Deng, Miao 200
denim
    Buckskin 59
    Iron Man 59
    Snobak pre-shrunk 15, 55, 59, 67, 69
dental plan 169
Department of Education 159
Department of Industry and
        Development 162, 163
Department of Regional Economic
        Expansion 165, 167

Depression 53, 56, 59, 61, 146
Dien, Qui 191
distribution 17, 112, 113, 146, 162, 163,
        173
Dotto, Assunta (Peron) 88, 100, 101
Downey, Lynn 152
Duce, Frank 140
Dupire, Serge 173

E
Earl, Gordon 140
Eaton's 59, 61, 164
Economic Development Edmonton 194
Economy Commercial Co. Ltd. 24
Edmonton AB 15, 16, 17, 19, 20, 21, 24, 25,
        26, 30, 34, 35, 37, 38, 39, 58, 59, 61, 88,
        98, 103, 105, 114, 118, 124, 125, 130,
        132, 134, 140, 143, 154, 155, 156, 158,
        159, 160, 162, 163, 164, 165, 167, 168,
        169, 170, 172, 179, 180, 182, 183, 184,
        185, 187, 188, 192, 193, 194, 195
    Special Relief Department 59
Edmonton: Alberta's Capital City 25
Edmonton and District Labour Council
        134, 159
Edmonton Bulletin 37, 41, 98, 102, 107
Edmonton Chamber of Commerce 93
Edmonton Free Press 33
Edmonton Journal 17, 21, 30, 61, 91, 97, 154,
        155, 159, 160, 161, 162, 164, 167, 169,
        170, 172
Edmonton Knitting Company 24
Edmonton Oilers 177
Edmonton Trades and Labour Council
        (ETLC) 20, 30, 34, 39, 131
Elk Point AB 125, 134
Emery Manufacturing 24
emphysema 131
engineers 98, 154
Engley, Nellie 88, 97, 99, 100
English in the Workplace 185, 186, 190
Esdale Press Ltd. 37, 43

Ethical Trading Action Group 188
Evening Journal 20
examiners 93, 125, 134

F
Factories Act 29, 30, 39
Faded Glory 164
Family Herald 65
Farm and Ranch Review 23, 26, 35
Farm Workshop Guide 66, 73, 147
Farmer's Advocate and Home Journal 35
farmers 15, 22, 28, 30, 35, 98, 102, 108, 124,
        128, 146
"Featured at Leading Stores across
        Canada" 124
Feng, Hui Fang 200
Feng, Yan Al 202
fire prevention 30
Fleming, Hertha 88
floor men 101
floor women 101, 102
Frank's Café 102
Frasch, August 26
Freeland, Don 152, 164, 167, 172

G
General Whitewear 54
George S. May International Co. 98
Gerlitz, Wilf 140
Gilbertson, Emma 88
Gill, Amandeep 200
Girard, Gilles 173
globalization 16, 133, 190
Global Success Sharing Plan 190
Gobeil, Larry 170
Godsoe, J. Gerald 93, 133, 151-152, 159,
        160
Goodis, Goldberg, Soren Ltd. 164
Gormley, Russell 160, 162, 165
government contracts 87, 88, 101, 106
Grace Lingerie Manufacturing Co. 24
Gradzi, Halina 202

Graham, Charles A. 15, 19, 30, 35, 53, 54, 88, 93, 152
Great Northern Apparel Inc. (GNA) 17, 170, 172
Great-West Life Assurance 116
Great Western Garment Company
  Almanac 96, 140, 141, 195, 197
  catalogues 50, 51, 68, 69, 70, 75, 77, 78, 81, 103, 105, 110, 119, 123, 136, 138, 146, 147, 171, 173, 195, 196, 198, 199
  distribution centre 163
  factories
    Brantford 17, 160, 161, 162, 164, 168, 169, 185, 187, 190, 193, 194
      Elgin Street 167, 168, 169, 170
    Cornwall 17, 172, 190, 192
    Edmonton 17, 179, 184, 185, 187, 188, 192, 193, 194
      86 Street and 106A Avenue 116, 117, 118, 126, 156, 158, 162, 164, 167, 172
      97 Street and 103 Avenue 30, 33, 42, 88, 89, 90, 95, 98, 102, 103, 107, 115
      105 Avenue and 97 Street 24, 25, 26, 27, 29
      4104-99 Street 167
      9616-101A Avenue 41, 43
    fire 41, 43
    Manitoba 162
    Saskatoon 17, 168, 172
      34 Street and Ontario Avenue 167, 168
    Stoney Creek 17, 172, 190, 192, 193, 194
    Winnipeg 17, 160, 161, 162, 164, 168, 172
      36 Bannatyne Avenue 168
  Household Handbook 137, 195, 197
  labels 109, 122
    UGWA 108
    Union Made 18, 21, 22, 39, 153
  logos 108, 122, 152, 157, 181

    Sanforized Shrunk 109, 122
    Union Made 122
  warehouses 160, 162, 163, 165
Gretzky, Wayne 176, 177
GWG (Eastern) Limited 164, 169
GWG Inc. 170, 172, 173
GWG Limited 164, 165, 169, 173

H
Haas, Melinda 88
Haas, Peter 133, 152, 169, 187, 188
Haas, Walter 133, 152
Hatch, Eileen 118, 126
He, Li Chan 200
health 93, 96, 130-131, 158, 169, 183-184, 186
  women's 184
Heath, Barb 183, 184, 185
Henderson's Directories 24
Hobden, Effie 98
Holland 103, 107
Hook, Norah 98, 105
Huang, Xin (Allan) Qiang 200
Hudson's Bay Company 56
Hungary 130, 183

I
IAAF World Championships in Athletics 192
immigrants 24, 26, 88, 100, 124-126, 128, 129, 130, 155, 156, 158, 159, 164, 168, 179-180, 182, 195
  American 24
  Cambodian 155, 158
  Chinese 129, 155, 156, 158, 179, 182, 185, 186, 187
  Czechoslovakian 158
  Dutch 124
  employees 88, 100, 164, 180, 195
  Filipino 168, 187
  German 124, 126
  Hong Kong 155

  Hungarian 124, 125, 130
  Indian 182, 185, 187
  Indo-Fijian 182
  Indo-Trinidadian 182
  Italian 88, 100, 124, 125, 126, 128, 182
  Laotian 155, 158
  Polish 124, 125
  Portuguese 124, 125, 182, 187
  Punjabi 129
  Ukrainian 88, 124-126, 128, 129
  United Kingdom 24
  Vietnamese 155, 156, 158, 159, 164, 168, 187
India 183
industrial accidents 54, 185
Ingram, Harriet J. 39
injuries 184, 185
  repetitive strain 184
instructors 39, 93, 99, 102, 131, 155, 158, 159, 180, 184
internees 106

J
Jack Spratt 192
jackets 55, 57, 58
  Cowboy King 64, 99, 103, 143
  Iron Man 57
  Ranch Boss 118
  Red Strap 58
  Shearling Lined 137
  Westwool 71, 138
Jackshirt 127
Jackson, Alfred E. 15, 19, 35, 36
Jacox, Clarence D. 53, 54, 88, 89, 90, 93, 97, 101, 114, 117, 133, 151
Jones, Iola 92
Jones, Ken 168

K
Kabesh, Louis 134, 152
Kays Overall Manufacturers 24

Kesler, Red 140
Kettner, Ben 160
Khan, Sadat 182,194
King, William Lyon Mackenzie 93
Kitchen Overall and Shirt Co..
      See Kitchen-Peabody Garments
      Limited
Kitchen-Peabody Garments Limited 160,
      161
Klapstein, Ellen (Cox) 92
Kozma, Elizabeth 130,183
Krewenchuk, Helen 154

L

L.W. Caldwell Ltd. 39
Labour Day 44,88
labour disputes 16
labour unions 18,20,21,22
labourers 15,130,146
Lacent Technologies Inc. 192
ladies' wear 16,17,115,123,124,146,172
LaFlèche Bros. 24,39-40
leather department 41,43
Leduc AB 120,124
Les Classels 173
Levi's 17,124,152,154,165,167,169,170,
      172,179,180,183,184,185,187,188,
      189,190,192,193,194
Levi's 488 Project 194
Levis Strauss 17,124,130,170,179,180,
      181,182,185,187,188,190,192,193,
      194,195
Levis Strauss Canada Inc. 170
Levi Strauss & Co. 133,152,157,160,164,
      165,167,169,172
Levi Strauss & Co. (Canada) Inc. 165,
      168,170
Lindsay ON 169
Livingstone, Alexander 33
Lloyd, Harry 177
London ON 169
Lone Ranger Club 145

long-term disability 169
lumbermen 22

M

mackinaw jackets 35,41,43
Maclean's 48,76,123,124,146,148,149,
      152
Mah, Chee Luck 156,192
Mah, Hang Sau 156
Mah, Virginia 155,156,158
management 15,16,17,18,20,21,22,31,
      34,61,91,93,96,97,100,101,113,114,
      117,118,125,131,133,134,151,152,
      153,160,167,168,169,170,172,181,
      186,187,189,190,193,194
Marathon Realty 162
marketing 17,124,136,140,146,164,170,
      177,179
   French-language 173
   radio 164
   television 164
maternity leave 40
maximum hours 39
Maxine School of Beauty Culture 39
May, Mike 160
Mayan, Esther 88
McCormack, James B. 24
McDermid Engraving Company 37
McDermid Studios 25,33
McIntyre, Arthur 54
McIntyre, Robert W. 54
McKinnon, R.H. 159
mechanics 21,22,28,34,93,100
Medeiros, Bernadette 202
medical insurance plan 129
Mennonite Centre for Newcomers 169
menswear 16,17,124,146,152,160,172
Menswear Magazine 165
Mertens, Erwin 169,172
Metropolitan Store 54
Mexico 190
miners 22,28,35

minimum wage 24,30,34,35,39,40,54,
      113,159
Minimum Wage Board 38,39
Mohawk College 187
Monthly Trade Letter 53
Montreal QC 16,20,26,164,173,192
Mooney, Marie 132
Morris, Cody 140
Morris, Lillian 38,39,61
Mothers' Allowance Act 40
Muttart Foundation 169

N

National Employment Service 158
National Film Board 94,95
National Home Monthly 65,146
National War Labor Board 99
Nattrass, Floyd 162
Nelson, Beulah 98
Netherlands. *See* Holland
New York NY 16,20,34,101,108,131,132,
      134,152,166,170
Ngo, Kim 194
Nijjar, Parminder 202
Nimis, Irma 100
North American Free Trade Agreement
      (NAFTA) 165,190,193
Northern Alberta Institute of Technology
      (NAIT) 159
Northern Mariana Islands 188
Northwestern Manufacturing 24,61
Nufer, E.C. 159
nursing 130,131,183-185

O

office workers 93
Olson, Carl 140
Ontario Development Corporation grant
      167
operators 21,24,29,30,34,35,41,42,54,
      57,87,88,89,93,94,98,99,100,102,
      106,114,115,118,125,126,130,131,

106, 114, 115, 118, 125, 126, 130, 131,
   152, 154, 158, 165, 167, 168, 172, 184,
   185, 188, 189-191
Orsini, Marina 173
outsourcing 16, 18, 39
overalls 22, 24, 28, 29, 37, 39, 41, 57, 58, 59,
   61, 103, 161
   Blue Diamond 37
   carpenter 127
   Railroad Signal 160
   Red Strap 47, 49, 51, 58, 65, 126, 139
Ozipko, Anne 88, 118, 130, 159, 161, 169,
   170, 172, 187

P

Pacific Coast Militia Regiment 106
packers 93
paid holidays 101
painters 22
Panama Canal 16
pants 21, 22, 24, 28, 31, 35, 39, 41, 54, 55, 57,
   58, 59
   black 35
   Bleach Out 164
   British Khaki 84
   Bum Bums 84, 171, 173
   Bum Jeans 84
   Cachet Cadet 84
   Canadian Wilderness Gear 84
   Cowboy King 64, 110, 115, 126, 141, 142,
      143
   Dockers 188, 192
   Drillers Drill 48, 76, 77, 120, 125
   Femme Fit 84, 85, 171, 173
   Flare Kings 84, 85
   Frisco Jeans 76, 77, 121, 124
   Frontier Queen 79, 121, 123
   George W. Groovey 82, 166
   Grace W. Groovey 83, 166
   Great Western Jeans 84
   GwGeans 175
   GWG Kings 81

High Rigger 134
Iron Man 57, 65, 67-68, 139
jeans 15, 17, 98, 110, 115, 122, 126, 134,
   140, 152, 154, 164, 165, 167, 168, 169,
   171, 172, 173, 188, 189, 190, 192, 193,
   194, 200, 202
Jeanslax 84
Kidfitters 84
Nev'R Press 82, 157
Odyssey 84, 173
Peace Jeans 16, 164, 165
Pionnier jeans 84
Poupounette jeans 84
Ranch Boss 118
Red Strap 48, 51, 58, 65, 139
Rugby 84
Scrubbies 15, 84, 164, 167, 173, 174, 194
Signature 193
Snobak 69
Softies 164
Springbok 60, 122
Strap Back 80
Strapbacks 123
Tradition of Excellence 84
Wash Out 164
parkas 138
   Shearling Lined 137
Patronize Local Industry 37
Peabody's Ltd.. See Kitchen-Peabody
   Garments Limited
Pearn, Dale 162, 172
pensions 93, 101
piecework 21, 33, 34, 40, 53, 54, 99, 100,
   131, 134, 151, 158, 170, 188, 189, 190
Pilichowsky, Able Seaman W. 106
pockets, Stop-Loss 54, 57
polio 130
Pontney, Lloyd 92
Popowich, Kay 134
pressers 93
price fixing 169
profit sharing 190

Provost AB 140

Q

Quinn, Charley 92, 94
quota system 188, 189

R

railwaymen 22, 35, 37
Ramsey's 24
Razga, Hana 158
Red Cross 130
Red Deer AB 160
refugees 106, 158
Regina SK 134, 140
Regional Labor Board 101
Reinbold, Jim 140
Revillon 19
Reynolds, Harold N. 23, 24, 54
Reynolds, Lloyd 54
Reynolds Manufacturing 24, 54
Rich, Abraham 160, 162
Rich, David 160, 161
Richlu Manufacturing 161
Ritchie, Bob 92
rivets 99, 110, 130, 202
Robinson, Bob 140, 143, 172
Rocky Mountain House AB 99
rodeos 140, 172
Romanuk, Mary 125
Roper, Elmer E. 30
Roscoe, Roger 160
Ross, Emily (Bullock) 99, 131, 133, 134
Ross, Jack 131
Ross, Tony 131
Royal Canadian Air Force 87, 103, 119
Royal Canadian Army 87, 100, 103
Royal Canadian Mounted Police (RCMP)
   100
Royal Canadian Navy 87, 106
Royal Commission on Price Spreads
   and Mass Buying. See Stevens
   Commission

S

safety 29, 30, 96, 183, 184, 186, 187, 191
Safety Stock Analysis Forecast and
    Earnings System (SAFE) 162
sales force 26, 93, 126, 162, 172
San Antonio TX 193
San Francisco CA 169, 187
Sanforized compressive shrinkage process
    59
Saskatoon SK 17, 167, 168, 172
Sauve, Virginia 185-187
seamstresses 21
Seattle WA 53, 93
sewing room 26, 29, 31
Shaw, W.B. 160
Shaw family 88, 152
Shinbine, Elizabeth 54
shirts 22, 24, 28, 30, 39, 53, 55, 62
    Blue Diamond 50, 72, 74
    Bushmaster 137
    Cowboy King 143
    Drillers Drill 48, 76, 120
    El Charro 74, 75
    Golden West Jean 67
    Graham Shirt 53
    Husky 60, 69, 122
    Palomino 78
    Pinto 75
    Sport Togs 74, 75, 127
    Texas Ranger 47, 60, 72-73, 141
    Zeromole 69
sick leave 169
Silva, Ana 170
slogans
    "Anything Goes" 166
    "History in the Making" 179, 181
    "I Grew Up in GWGs" 176, 177
    "J'ai grandi avec GWG" 176
    "Made in Alberta" 40
    "Made in the West for the West" 26, 136
    "Shop Locally" 40
    "They wear longer because they're made
        stronger" 35, 36
    "Union Made" 153
Smith, Bill 194
smocks
    Red Strap 51
snaps 110
sportswear 17, 113, 146
St. John Ambulance 158
Stanfield's 162
Star Weekly 46, 49, 67, 80, 119, 120, 123,
    124, 146, 147, 148, 149
statutory holidays 114
Stephens, Doug 119
Stephenson, Annie 39, 90, 101
Stevens, Harold 59
Stevens Commission 59
Stoney Creek ON 17, 168, 172, 190, 192,
    193, 194
Strathcona AB 24
Strathcona Industrial Park 162, 167
strikes 20, 190
supervisors 125, 126, 130, 158, 180, 183
suspender slide, Lochbar 54
sweatshops 16, 18, 20, 21, 61, 158, 182, 188
Swift Current SK 140

T

Tagliente, Giuseppina 182
Tan Holdings Corporation 188
Taylor, R 159
tendonitis 131
ticket system 99
Tigeris, Chris 183, 184, 185
Tilley Press Building 43
Tilley Press Ltd. 41
time engineers 118, 131
Tools for School 181
Toronto ON 16, 20, 26, 30, 34, 124, 133,
    151, 160, 161, 164, 170, 172, 173, 187,
    193

Trades and Labour Congress 134
training 158, 159, 164, 167, 168, 169, 180,
    184, 194
Tran, Chi 202
Tran, Lien 200
Triangle Shirtwaist Factory fire 20
Trivett, Grace 97
tuberculosis 98, 130
Tuberculosis Act 98

U

Unemployment Insurance Board of
    Referees 170
uniforms
    dress 87
    explosive workers 87
    military 17, 87, 103
    militia units 106
    prisoner-of-war 17, 87, 106
    Royal Canadian Navy 106
unionization 20, 22
unions, garment 16
United Food and Commercial Workers
    International Union (UFCW) 190
    Apparel, Garment, and Textile Workers
        Council 190
United Garment Workers of America
    (UGWA) 18, 20, 21, 22, 26, 34, 40, 61,
    190
    Local 120 20, 30, 34, 35, 39, 40, 44, 88, 93,
        96, 97, 98, 99, 100, 101, 108, 113, 114,
        117, 126, 131, 132, 133, 134, 151, 152,
        153, 157, 159, 170, 172, 180, 184, 186,
        194
    Local 486 168
United Garment Workers of Canada
    (UGWA)
    Local 120 118
United States 152, 153, 165, 172, 188, 190,
    193
United Way 181

United States 152, 153, 165, 172, 188, 190, 193
United Way 181

V

vacation 114
Vancouver BC 16, 162
Victory Bonds 97, 98
Vietnam 187
Vietnam War 165

W

wages 39, 54, 61, 92, 93, 99, 101, 114, 131, 133, 134, 155, 158, 189, 190
Waggott, Emily (Gale) 43, 59
Wal-Mart 193
Walker, Beverly 185, 186
War Records-Manufacturing (WRM) 95
wartime contracts 30
Wartime Information Board 95
Wartime Prices and Trade Board 93, 101
Wasylynchuk, Lillian 130
Watson, Roberta (Walsh) 54
welfare 93
Western boosterism 17
Western Linen 169
Wetaskiwin AB 160
Williams, Beulah (Nelson) 92
Williamson, Percy 94
Windsor ON 134
Winnipeg MB 16, 17, 26, 114, 153, 160, 162, 163, 164, 168, 170, 172, 195
Winnipeg General Strike 35
Winnipeg Pants Manufacturing Company 160, 162
women
   as employees 21, 24, 29, 34, 38, 40, 54, 88, 92, 93, 98, 101, 125, 130, 159, 164, 180, 187, 195
   in union 38, 39
Wong, Mai Fung 202
Wong, Mai Mui 200

Wong, Nancy 194
Wong, Sum Yuk 156, 158
Woodward's 140, 143
Woolworth 174
work hours 30, 39, 40, 61, 184, 194
work sharing program 190
workers 15, 16, 17, 18, 20, 21, 22, 24, 26, 30, 31, 34, 35, 36, 37, 39, 40, 41, 42, 44, 54, 59, 61, 87, 88, 93, 95, 96, 97, 98, 99, 100, 101, 102, 105, 107, 113, 114, 117, 118, 124, 125, 128, 129, 130, 131, 133, 134, 151, 155, 156, 157, 158, 159, 160, 161, 162, 164, 167-168, 169, 170, 172, 179-180, 181-183, 184, 185-187, 188, 189-190, 192-193, 194
   non-unionized 22
   unionized 18, 93, 108, 152, 168
workforce 19, 21, 25, 26, 29, 33, 35, 88, 98, 103, 115, 118, 124, 129, 155, 156, 160, 162, 168, 172, 179, 187, 190, 192
working conditions 22, 24, 27, 30, 31, 33, 39, 61, 93, 98, 99, 101, 130, 131, 188, 190, 194
Workmen's Compensation 184
workwear 16, 17, 35, 54, 59, 87, 112, 113, 146
   Beavertail 60, 76
   Blue Diamond 70
   boys' 17
   Cachet Cadet 173
   Cowboy King 46, 54, 55, 59, 64, 118, 142, 143, 152, 156, 157
   Driller's Drill 76, 120, 124
   El Charro 71, 75
   Frisco Jean 46
   Frontier Queen 46, 76, 79, 123, 124, 146
   George W. Groovey 16, 76, 82
   Golden West Jean 64, 69
   Grace W. Groovey 16, 76, 83
   Graham 76
   GWG Kings 76, 81, 152, 156
   High Rigger 76, 124, 134

   Husky 54, 60, 67, 69
   Iron Man 54, 57, 65, 66, 67-68, 157
   ladies' 17
   men's 16, 17
   Nev'R Press 76, 82
   Palomino 76, 78
   Peace Jeans 76
   Pinto 71, 74
   Plonnier 173
   Poupounette 173
   Ranch Boss 76, 118, 122, 124
   Red Strap 54, 58, 59, 64, 65
   Sport Togs 64
   Springbok 60, 76, 122, 124
   Strapback 76, 124, 146
   Texas Ranger 46, 54, 60, 62, 69, 72-73
   Westwool 68, 70
work week 30, 39, 101, 114, 194
World's Largest Jeans 192-193
World War I 17, 26
World War II 17, 24, 56, 59, 64, 87, 88, 92, 93, 100, 101, 103, 106, 119, 128, 146, 152
Wrangler 172

Y

Yan, Ai Yi 200
Yeandle, Ilene 126, 130, 131, 158

Z

zippers 110, 200
   Lightning 110

ABOUT THE AUTHOR

Catherine C. Cole is the editor of *Inventive Spirit: Alberta Patents from 1905-1975*, Red Deer and District Museum, 1999, and co-author with Judy Larmour of *Many and Remarkable: The Story of the Alberta Women's Institutes*, Alberta Women's Institutes, 1997.

On the subject of GWG, she wrote "Working Conditions in Edmonton's Garment Manufacturing Industry, 1911-1945," in *Edmonton: The Life of a City*, B. Hesketh & F. Swyripa, eds., Edmonton and District Historical Society, 1995; *The Great Western Garment Company, 1911-1939: "Who Threw the Overalls in Mrs. Murphy's Chowder?"* Alberta Museums Association, Occasional Paper 1, 1989; and "Garment Manufacturing in Edmonton, 1911-1939," MA Thesis, University of Alberta, 1988.